THE LAST PRIESTESS

The true story of the temple and Solomon.

By Luna Ora
& The Sisters of The Temple

THE LAST PRIESTESS

I will always be your voice, sisters.

In every time, space, and dimension.

Your transmutation gave me new codes of power and opened a new portal for us all to awaken from, into a new dream...

You are free now and forever to dance wildly under the moon, to run naked under the sun and to make love to your God in the sacred waters of the Temple.

This book is dedicated to the sisters who have lost their lives by the demonic forces, on October 2023, in Israel,

and to all the sisters who carry the flames of life, truth, and love.

True sisterhood will save this world.

WE ARE LIFE.

LUNA ORA

Mother Is Rising
The sex magic school of ISIS and LILITH.
Luna Ora
motherisrising@gmail.com
www.motherisrising.com

Written and channeled by: Luna Ora
and the sisters of the temple.

Disclaimer

This book is provided by Mother Is Rising for educational or entertainment purposes only.

None of this content is intended to offer, or replace, qualified medical or health related advice.

The author accepts no responsibility or liability whatsoever for any injury, loss or damage in any shape or form incurred in part or in whole as a direct or indirect result of use or reliance upon the information and material presented here.

ספר זה מוקדש ללבנה
שגם בשמי הלילה
מאירה את דרכנו חזרה הביתה

SPECIAL THANKS

This book is dedicated to all my sisters in all time and space. Especially to the sisters of the Temple who are still alive and safe, thriving with their power as they speak to me throughout dreams and the womb of the Mother.

It is also dedicated to my sisters in this lifetime, those who know and love me for all that I am as well as to the priestesses that have been initiated and those who are on their way back home…

To Liat and Lilach. My inner girl will always love you. you have kept your love and friendships no matter how far I fly in other worlds.

To Varya for always being my grounding home, Mahyar, Sueanne, Simona & Andreanne, who truly see me. To McKenzie, Lisa, Tabea, Pryia, Leena, Yoni, Nataly, and Lila.

To my brother Obada. I'm so happy I found you in this life again.

To all the soul family that has come and gone and those who will soon cross my path. You all inspire me and push me to grow in your endless ways.

A special deep gratitude to my familiar Luna, who has given me my priestess's name and reminded me the love of a home.

The sweetest thanks are dedicated to my earthly mother, Michaela. Your courage and power have given me mine.

CONTENT

THE LAST PRIESTESS
The true story of the temple and Solomon.

By Luna Ora &
The Sisters of The Temple

"To those of you who can still see the dragons. Those fierce, loving guardians who came to us, brought us back to life and guarded us, in our new realm, until this day, when we could call you again, sister, and ask you to bring our truth back to this lost world. We chose you not only because you were the last of us to live once before, but because your inner fire matches that of those dragons, who have always protected our wisdom and the temple."
- Your sisters from a Temple far within you.

PREFACE

Before I even remembered that I was ever a sex priestess, something always drew me to the darkness of this reality, and especially in men. The idea of bringing their darkness into light repulsed and attracted me at the same time. Natural Desire for exploration and one of my biggest subconscious goals. Ever since I was a young girl, even before I ever understood what sex was, I knew what sexual energy was. Even before I knew anything about men or relationships, I knew the power and I understood how the sexual sacred union energies work. You can say that I just naturally knew how magic works, and my realm of expertise was always naturally within the sexual arena.

My earthly father was a pure embodiment of the dark masculine.

So was *he*. Let's call him the man of chaos.

One man in particular.

A man that was so dark. That he has given me all the secrets to unlock my own power and potential as a priestess, as well as understanding the darkness within men. Within the masculine, so that I can transmute it and so that I can teach other women how to do so as well.

For years, that was my mission. To purposefully surround myself with this darkness so that I could become stronger because of it. Knowingly I did so. I was not a stupid girl who just allowed a man who was dark to hurt her. I have always walked into it with a full knowing, power, and control, while at the same time relinquishing control so that I may completely be in my divine feminine and learn all the light codes that this experience with this darkness of a man could teach me in this physical body. For those of you who are born with the codes of the sex priestess, it is very easy to understand these words. Even if you don't logically understand them, you know them in your body. You know my experience because even if you haven't dealt with these energies directly yourself, you have desired to in some way or another. Now that I remember my story and I remember my lifetime from the temple and I feel my rage as I bring up the image of Solomon raping and murdering my sisters, I understand exactly why I've always desired this experience in this current lifetime. Why I was so drawn to take upon myself this utterly difficult and draining mission of fighting with the darkest masculine possible. I wanted to prove to the sisters and to the mother that I can handle this darkness and that I have the power and the wisdom to transmute it and awaken the masculine and this reality into the light, into his heart. But mostly, I probably wanted to prove this power to myself after being so powerless in the days of the fall of the temple. My temple. Our temple.

There came a point where this darkness took too much out of me. It happened after my abortion. Getting pregnant from this darkest man I had met in this life was all the limit that I could take. I have communicated with this child's soul. Long before it came into my body, and we are still communicating until today. This child was never meant to be born; this child was a gift. From the mother, and it gave me the gift of full power, of understanding how to work and manipulate and transmute those dark masculine energies into love. The sexual union with the darkest of masculine I could find in this world was the biggest gift that I got as a sex priestess, because it formed inside me a new life. The purest of magic possible. A child. An alchemical child that, for me, will be forever the portal that showed me the ultimate ways of transmutation of utter shadow into pure light.

The sisters have shown me, throughout time and my initiation, that the more I connected to the temple and to them, that I do not need to allow such dark masculine energies inside me anymore. Now it is my time of pure self-love. Self-devotion. Now it is time to remember I am sacred. And now I can transmute these energies in other ways than hurt myself directly by sexually uniting with this dark, masculine force. Now I have the knowledge. I have wisdom. And above all, I have love. The love for the mother, for the sisters, and mainly for me.

I do not have to lie with demons any longer, for my demons work for me. For I can harness, control, and manipulate any demonic force on this planet. I am a sister of the temple. I do not fear bathing in shadow, and because of that, I have the powers to bring tremendous amounts of light.

I want you to repeat this last sentence now, sister, out loud. Repeat it as many times as you need to feel the power of these words:

"My demons work for me. For I am capable of harnessing, controlling, and manipulating any demonic force on this planet. I am a sister of the temple. I do not fear bathing in shadow, and because of that, I have the powers to bring tremendous amounts of light."

Did these words resonate with anything in you?
Remember who you are, sister.

Come back to the temple.

No matter the path you take, it is your inevitable right - for you ARE the temple, and you hold it within you forever.

Now that I understand that a deeper part of me always remembered the sacrifice taken from my sister's blood, I understand my yearning desires to play with the forbidden, to make Love with a monster. Now I understand how I've always had the natural ability and understanding to dive into my shadow and the deepest, ugliest darkness possible. Because this is where my power was the whole time. And now that I have brought the memories of the fall of the temple and the fall of my sisters out from my own deepest shadows, I am ready. Like never before.

I do not have to pay the price with the dark masculine any longer.

I do not have to pay with my body and blood. We have already paid the price of the dark masculine sacrifice for too long, and now it is not only women, but men as well who yearned for us to awaken sisters. This world needs the light codes of the temple once more, and they can only come through the most Powerful. Women. Alive!

Each moon, I let my blood flow on the walls of the temple where my sisters' sacrificial blood was forcefully drawn.

This blood of life freely given from the womb of the mother through our bodies is the eternal connection to her and to our own power and wisdom. Allow your blood to connect you with the temple as you read these memories of the time of the fall of the temple.

Perhaps you were in the temple with me, or perhaps you were in a land far away, doing your own work in your own way. Perhaps you were a tree or a medicinal flower in that realm, or even a cat. Perhaps you were a spirit guide, floating through time and space at that moment when I woke up to death around me, but either way, we all felt the pain. Of the cutting knife through our skin and hearts and we all felt the betrayal of the dark masculine we have loved and trusted.

It is a story repeating itself through ages, over and over again because of the trauma we all carry deep within us, sisters, that started within the walls of the temple, but really began before time existed, as the first masculine force abandoned the mother herself and separated himself from her…

We are the only ones who can stop the cycle of this story to ever be repeated. We are the ones who can birth the new world of the mother, so we must rise. And this raising of our power is a full surrender to it. It is not a forceful desire for control as the dark masculine. It is a yearning to return home and to bring all the children of the mother back home with us. It is the delicate whisper that you're hearing inside your soul right now reading these words that awakens the memories of who you are once more in your body. In the next few days, allow your body to move, shake., sing., dance., fuck. Do whatever it needs to do to release these memories you are about to read and transmute them into the present moment. Allow your own light codes to be unstuck as memories and emotions flood your being.

(For those of you who were triggered by the word 'fuck' I invite you to explore why it was so triggering? What are your perceptions, labels, and beliefs about this word and what it brings up for you? Know that within the safe, endless space of the sacred union, fucking is a way of life, an art form of the endless expressions of love.)

Uniting with the demons of the dark masculine has given me endless wisdom, but it also took my inner divine feminine grace, for I had to be a constant warrior and a protector of my sanity, body, and spirit. Now that I have my full power, I do not need any more of this war. I do not need to fight the dark masculine or myself. I remember who I am, and I know exactly what to do. My dark goddess, my divine feminine loving warrior, my raging bitch, and my innocent girl from every lifetime now stepping aside and allowing space to a peaceful priestess within me. For the earth witch. For the mother that holds everyone within her womb with love.

All these aspects of my divine feminine are necessary and are all a gift. When was your warrior in charge? Is she just waking up now after a long slumber? Was she ever allowed to rage at all? Or, like me, is she feeling it's time for her to rest and allow another aspect of your inner goddess to take over?

Thank you.

PART 1

WHO I AM NOW

CHAPTER 1

I come from the world of the three moons and on the 6th night of the 6th month I vanished from my world into this one. You call this childbirth.

Reincarnation. For you it may seem like the beginning of my journey as I am immersed here from a woman's body, as a baby, but for me it is only one step in a long everlasting journey.

I forgot. Like everyone does.

I forgot who I was and where I came from. I was born into a home, into a space that is misfortunate to say, very common in this world. An abusive, absent father. A mother who is too powerful, too demanding, too loud, but also very loving, can drive any child to madness, really. Being raised and nourished by a person who holds such anger and pain and yet such love at the same time, who can beat you in one moment and hug you the next. It would have been easier if my mom would just have been a lunatic, but she was all of it. She was the good and the bad. She was both my love and my fear. She was the power that I got as a woman and everything that I did not want to become. Perhaps another layer to my enigma is this woman who gave birth to me. Her own inner split reflects the split of my soul to always be yearning for home and never being able to stop moving and searching for it. This is where my story begins and where it ends as well, I suppose. In the search for a home. Perhaps I will always be searching, or until I return to the temple, I hope, after this life ends.

Some people call me a priestess. Some call me a crazy woman. Some call me a vegan, some call me evil, some see me as a saint, some call me nothing. Perhaps I am everything. Perhaps I'm only a reflection of you. Whoever is listening to this story with their hearts, whoever is reading these words. Perhaps I am simply a yearning for one of your endless eternal aspects of the one mind we all share, in this endless space we call reality. Perhaps you are the one writing these words as you read them. Perhaps I am channeling one part of who *you* truly are. And perhaps- I am simply a mad woman, as they call me, and you are just reading my story after all.

Either way, what fun.

As I am sitting in a hotel room in Bangkok on the 5th floor beginning to tell my Tale, I can feel the blood dripping between my legs as it melts into the white towel that I placed on the chair earlier today even before I knew my blood will arrive. In any case, I love sitting naked in my room, so a towel would be a good idea.

I mean, who knows who else sat on this chair before me? I wouldn't want my pussy to touch unholy grounds.

I still hold within me the knowledge of my sisters. Like the divine mother herself, I, her daughter, her servant, and embodiment in a human form- birth new life for myself. As I bleed from my womb- her womb, I am, like all my sisters, a part of the endless cycle of her love. The blood nourishes me, and I nourish her back. I pray my blood will always run from between my legs, that it will never end, so I can offer it back to the mother until my last breath.

It's been 20 years now that I have been on the move. Of course, I was always a gypsy, but I had to play the normal life of a girl raised in a home, in a country, with an absent father and a mother who is too loud. And so I stayed there until I was old enough to leave.

Until I was brave enough to leave.

Two heavy bags and very little money and my 19-year-young taking flight.

Obviously, the entire tale of my life would be a pleasure for anyone who will read it, but after 20 years of being 'lost in the desert', as my Hebrew ancestors would call it, I am here in this hotel room in Bangkok realizing that no matter where I go and no matter how far I run, I can never run from myself. And I vow to not leave this hotel room until I tell my story because it's only when I tell it and birth it into life can I start to really live here and now.

Maybe because it is not only my story. It is the story of all my sisters, and a story that is connected to the fate of this entire world. So, it is your story as well. Whether you believe it or not, or whether you choose to use the information I am about to reveal in any way, is up to you.

There once was an Israelite king famous for his control over demonic spirits. He was a sorcerer. A dark wizard. One of many who will grow to expand and distort their powers over our world.

The seal of Solomon wasn't his. He stole it from us.

What if religion itself was created by dark wizards who had knowledge of real magic but wanted to keep it to themselves as well as control the masses with it? What a horrific, smart way to do so… to seed so much fear in humanity, so much trauma. To preach of a mysterious 'god' while punishing and shaming all that will not follow their control as they themselves practice demonic magic in plain sight? How weak does the human mind have to be to fall for this?

Well, a mind so weak was created as such. By ages of consuming animals, raping women and children, and using sexuality in the lowest forms - these 2 tools of shadow (food and sex) have lowered humanity's consciousness to a point where they are that weak, and even so dumb that they will follow just about anyone... and any story.

What is the difference in the story the dark wizards told humanity then and the one I am telling you now? Well, whether it is true or not, at least you can rest assured that mine has a small ingredient in it called - love....

PART 2

THE LAST DAY OF THE TEMPLE

CHAPTER 2

Today, it is not the peaceful pleasure of my body melting into my bed that wakes me up. It is not a pleasant dream, as always. I am waking up into a nightmare. Although I have never had a nightmare before or would even know what one is. I had lived within the sacred, safe walls of the temple my whole life, held, and caressed by all the sisters that live around me. So safe and eternally healed by the beauty and love of the Divine Mother herself.

Every day of my life is a ritual, every breath is gratitude, every step I take is of pleasure. But this day- I wake up to a nightmare. I wake up to hear my sisters scream. I have heard the marvelous, loud sounds of their yearning pleasure, their extasy, as they unite with the brothers of the temple or when they are deep in a rapturous dance, but I have never heard sounds like these from their voices before. My body cannot move, but something inside of me tells me to get up, and so I do.

I reach for my gown and cover my naked body.

Barefoot, I run in the corridors of the Temple. The screams make me dizzy as I hold onto the magical, carved walls and try to touch the endless spiral symbol of the womb, lit by a single candle, but I slip...

I feel the wetness underneath my left foot. I'm trying to see what it is because the corridor is dark and the pain in my left arm is too strong from falling. I grab my left arm with my right one and I let out scream I never had before when I see the blood on my foot. I cover my mouth, feeling I shouldn't allow my voice to reveal where I am. The silent voice inside me tells me to get up. Again.

So, I do.

As fast as I can.

That voice is all I have right now because I do not know who I am anymore in this chaos of blood and agony and fear of my sisters. I don't see their faces, but I felt a few of their bodies as I try to make my way through the shadows. Even if I don't see them, I feel them. We are all connected; you see. Me and all my sisters. We feel each other's dreams, desires, thoughts. We are one body, one ocean, moving as a multitude of waves, each one a miracle and a world of her own, but we are all one.

Sharing one womb, one breath. One love.

I keep running on the lifeless bodies around me. I know the sight of blood because they have taught me what sacred blood is. The same blood that one day will run freely from my body. The same blood that I saw flowing between my sister's legs each month, as they bled together, and I could not wait for the day that my blood will come as well so I can join them.

Seeing all the blood around me now, I'm not so sure anymore that I would like it. But then again- this blood, that I feel as heavy as thick mud on my feet now, like an evil force, weighing me down as it dries too quickly, suffocating my ankle as I try to move faster - is not the blood freely given. This is a blood taken. Taken from my sisters. By force. By hate. I know what hate is, not because I have ever felt or witnessed it. I know it because I can smell it in the air all around, and a part of me simply knows the face of it. A part of me begins to feel it as well, like an unstoppable monster growing inside of my chest. I've seen monsters before, although I am still young to go down to the lower parts of the temple and have never yet participated in the rituals of other worlds, some of my older sisters told me and showed me, the many creatures, and monsters they have encountered when they traveled to the other worlds. They have told me stories about hate. About what hate does to some and the monsters they create from their hate. I had always imagined hate as a monster because of their stories. I had always seen hate as a slow sipping thick fire that moves solely but tares someone from the inside. One day, they may allow me to travel to other worlds once I complete my initiation, unless they assign me the role of a healer or a guard. But I hope I will be a union priestess. I too wish to experience the pleasure and extasy of my sisters. I too want to travel to other worlds, but I know that whatever the mother needs me to embody, I shall, with pleasure.

I wonder now if I will ever even finish my initiation, or am I to fall dead to the ground like my sisters are now?

How selfish that all I can think of now is my initiation. I gasp as a hand clasps my ankle. It is Hania. She is laying, blood dripping from her mouth. I bend down to hold her face as she tries to say something, but she cannot even take a whole breath and her face falls to my palm, her eyes remaining open, as if they do not wish to leave like the rest of her. I cry, my hand still holding her gentle face, and when I pull my hand away, her ear jewel is caught in my ring, refusing to leave me. For some reason, it sends shivers down my spine and my first instinct is to pull her jewel and leave it there, but I choose to take it with me. A part of me feels she left me with a part of her to keep me company because I am all alone. Alive, walking along the endless lifeless bodies of the priestesses of the land of three moons.

I don't even know how many times I slip on the blood. I don't even know where I'm going. I am just crawling. Reminding myself to breathe as I'm looking for any sister, anyone who is still alive.

I still hear screams from far away. Perhaps they are in the lower or higher corridors above me, but all I can do, the coward that I am, is to hide in the first nuke that I find. Covering my head with my robe, as if the fabric will protect me from what is going on. Sitting here, covered in my sister's blood, not yet received my own blood, cowardly waiting. Waiting for someone to rescue me, to tell me what's going on, to wake me up from this dream, from this nightmare which I still don't know how to even name.

That was me. That little girl is still me. She has a reason to run, and perhaps she is the reason I am still running away, and I cannot find one place to rest peacefully on this entire planet. Even as the grown-ass adult woman that I am, even when this sacred blood is dripping between my legs now. Even though we are worlds apart, we still feel each other's pain. Through the womb, through time and space. I wish to come to peace with that little girl so that I may rest and find a home of my own, at the age of 39, I feel tired already. The gypsy in me is tired. She has taken me so far, but now, a new version of me is asking to guide the way.

You see, I am one of the sisters of the Temple. I am the one who survived, and it is up to me to keep and guard the teachings and the knowledge of the Temple and bring it to this new world that I live in right now. A world with an absent father and a mother who is too loud.

CHAPTER 3

In the days of the Temple, sacred unions between man and woman were of the ordinary. Of course, my sisters always taught me that no sacred Union is ordinary. In fact, our entire lives were surrounded by the path of the Sacred Union. But here in this world where animals are being tortured and killed each day, where everything's sacred turns to shit, I still must find the courage to bring the knowledge of Sacred Union into life. Good luck with that...

How the fuck am I supposed to do that? What a crazy path I am now faced with. In a world where people just fuck each other over for fun and literally just fuck each other, with no real connection of love or respect, I am supposed to preach of the power of true sexuality and love? In a world where children are being raped and murdered, where a father rapes his own daughter and a mother sells her own child for money, I am supposed to talk about sacredness and rituals in our everyday lives? In a world where sacred creatures are slaughtered for palate pleasure, I am supposed to teach about magic? Where wealth is being measured by how many items you have instead of how respectful you are to the land around you. How the fuck am I supposed to keep anything sacred in this kind of world? It feels like I've been fighting ghosts for the last 6 years, trying to teach the knowledge of the temple to humanity. I've written books, given workshops, and also have a YouTube channel where I share knowledge (what I can). But humanity is not ready. People seek the fast-track to immediate pleasure, the left path of shadows and ego and not the right path of initiation. Even the spiritual folks just want the easy way and will pay, follow, and worship those who offer them the illusion of reaching 'enlightenment'. How am I supposed to compete with the beautiful lies? With the fakeness of our culture, where all I have to offer is truth and a path that demands actual work and commitment? A path that asks for maturity from a generation who wants to stay a child.

And so here I am, about to become a woman of 40, in a hotel room in Bangkok, asking for redemption from that little girl who still had no power. So, as my sacred blood flows between my legs, I will tell our story. I will share the truth. I will be the big sister she needed to find in those bloody corridors. I will share the tale of us, and, perhaps, some may still see it as only a story, which is perfectly fine, but this story is going to light up pieces of you that you know are truth. And truth is everything that the temple was made for. Truth is everything that I am made for.

And so, truth is all that matters.

As long as you keep your heart open when you read this, your mind can remain closed. Trust that this 'tale' will speak to your heart and ignite the temple within you in the way you need it to.

If you remain with an open heart, *that* is a promise.

CHAPTER 4

The temple always had many snakes. No one ever got bitten. Snakes did not bite in the temple. They were a part of the land, the energy we all co-created together, and they held codes we received and moved through the portals, our own bodies and one another. The snakes held the codes that transferred between the temple itself and the consciousness of us- the sisters. They were our guide, healers, holders of wisdom. The snakes had their own paths and moved in a never-ending dance, twirling as life does, according to the needs of the temple. The snakes loved swimming in the sacred pool of green and blue that we all bathed in, more magnificent than anything I have still to witness on this modern plane. The sacred pool of green and blue was a place for the sisters only as well as the new mothers who gave birth at the temple. A place of life, of joy, peace, serenity, and calm.

But the sacred pool of green and blue - is now painted in red.

Let me tell you about my big sister. I will name her promethea to honor who she really was and keep her sacredness protected and pure in all lifetimes, in any dimensions she may be right now. Her name is not to be revealed, but to be worshiped and honored.

Promethea, *one* of my big sisters I mean, because all the women of the temple were my big sisters.

My birth mother brought me to the temple. I was brought as an offering to the Divine Mother herself because she knew that I had a higher calling. She heard the call of the Temple to bring me forth while I was still in her womb. This may seem odd to you in your world, and perhaps some of you may believe that I should be angry at my mother for giving me up so easily, how could she, right?

But in the time of the temple, in that reality we lived in, things were much simpler, yet much more magnificent and purer. Magic was a part of our daily lives. We lived Magic. My mother was very connected and highly attuned to source, as most women were. Even those who were not serving the temple itself directly served the mother and the divine in their own unique ways. My birth mother saw herself as a daughter of the Divine Mother herself, connected to all life and in service to the highest good, and so she gave me as an offering to the temple, knowing that my life would be as loving and safe as she would have given me, but her calling was to be with the land and the animals, and she knew that my soul craved for something higher. She was my vessel to arrive at the world and we both honored the agreements we had made when she created me and welcomed me into her. She knew my path was different from hers.

She was right.

The only problem is that I didn't get a chance to fully follow through with my initiation within the temple because the dark Wizards brutally murdered my sisters before I could do so.

I am very much aware that even writing the word 'wizard' may seem so odd, especially by a woman who is in her almost 40s sitting naked in a Bangkok hotel room. But you must understand, I am no ordinary woman. Neither are any of my sisters. So, let's get on with the tale, shall we?

Getting back to my old sister, let's call her P for short. I remember the day when she will come to him in the temple. I remember when he walked in. He looked very beautiful, charming, and tall. And I immediately felt her pull towards him even though I could not yet explain it as the girl that I was. I felt her, as I felt them all. Something in her changed when she saw him. It was like a wave of powerful force pulled her entire being towards him, and she didn't resist it. Why would she? It felt like Ecstasy. Like the pleasure we all lived for, and no one saw what he truly was. We never encountered such evil before, at least not in our world, only in others we traveled to, and his illusion was beyond enchanting.

Even though we all knew that she felt something for him, she did not dishonor the rites of initiation. She gave him no shortcuts and did not make it easier for him. He had to go through the entirety of six full moons to be purified within the external caves of the Temple. This is what I call the space, which is outside of the temple but still within it. It is the space where men go through cleansing and preparation before they're even allowed to enter the temple at all. They are brought food and shelter by the brothers of the Temple but they are still not allowed to fully walk into the temple until they are worthy of it and have been fully initiated, prepared, and mastered the ways of the temple. This is only the first key to their initiation, which takes many more moons and **cycles of sacred blood.**

This man. This tall, handsome man who we all felt was very powerful - brought to the downfall of all of us. But it wasn't just him. There were many like him, you see, many who have been seeking the powers of the goddess, the powers that only women can hold - which bring another strange dichotomy into our story, don't it? Because these dark forces, evil wizards, that have been controlling both of our worlds, have been wanting something that they can never actually have, and can never fully hold, bringing to the downfall of all of us. Causing so much chaos and bloodshed as they go.

I cannot let all this Blood shed be for vein, so let's continue with the story even though I know I sound like a proper lunatic to you by now.

CHAPTER 5

So, this man, this tall, handsome, powerful man, fooled us all.

As all the other men within the caves of the Temple, after a few months of living together and serving them, he felt like family. Many of them told us stories from the outside world, and I loved listening. But as I was serving him food every day, he was serving me lies, and like my sisters and brothers, I ate it all up.

You may think we are stupid or naïve, but we couldn't have known.

You see, such cruelty and evilness did not exist in our world, and I'm not just talking about our safe world within the walls of the Temple. The world we lived in was a peaceful one. It was a gentle world where the people lived sacredly with the land. I guess that in your modern terms, one label you will use for us is vegans. Yes, we did not consume animals. We did not consume death, pain, or fear. We practiced the highest form of white magic (in human terms). Magic that works with the forces of life, love, and unity. Magic that moves *with* life and not against it. That is exactly why the world we lived in was so peaceful, safe, and loving. The world where sacred unions were a thing of the ordinary. Where Magic existed in our every breath. Where many creatures whom you would consider mythical and magical existed alongside us.

But this man, and all the other dark Wizards took that away from us.

It is not easy for me to write the story as I sit in this Bangkok hotel room. I must take many breaks to catch my breath and hold myself steady. As I dictate my voice into the speech note, my left hand seems to have a mind on its own as it clenches so hard, I can't control it. I just allow the clenching in my left hand to be. Luckily, I cut my nails yesterday so that I don't hurt myself because I would probably dig into my skin if I had long nails, and I was blessed with very tough nails.

As I tell this tale, and as I remember it, my left hand cannot stop clenching. I don't know when I will stop. Perhaps when I finish telling this tale? So, I better get a move on because my hand is starting to hurt.

Luckily, I don't have to use my hands to write. I'm using my voice. In this machine called a laptop I sit in front of, that dictates everything I say. It feels right. It feels like this story should be told by my voice. This story should be spoken by the voice of a sister who has witnessed the bloodshed, in that world and this one. And whether you think that this is a lie or simply a story, I will sit here with a clenched hand as I breathe courage into my voice to keep speaking.

Truth. Is all I live for.

CHAPTER 6

I vowed to not leave this hotel room until the entire story is told and I'm running out of drinking water.

I remember the day when that man, that tall, handsome lie, was given permission to enter the temple. It was me who asked for the honor to wash his feet before he walked into the sacred halls of our.....

I'm sorry…. The anger inside of me just won't stop. I need to take a breath.

I can't fucking believe that I asked for the honor to wash this man's feet, believing his every lie. Believing he was worthy of entering the most sacred space on our Earth. Perhaps this is the clenching in my hand. This deep agonizing guilt that I'm feeling… This anger towards myself. Perhaps if I had not washed his feet… if I had not been the one to smile at him as he so viciously….

But I did. And I can't change that. All I can do is keep telling the story, hoping for some redemption. I suppose that the fact that I was still alive means something. It *must* mean something.

Feeling that the fate of an entire world lays in my hands. My stupid hands that washed his feet...I am disgusted. I know this is a silly thought. I know I am not the one to blame and that I merely served my duty in the temple. We greeted with honor each man and woman who wished to enter and unite with the temple. By washing a stranger's feet, we humble ourselves as sacred servants and offer an example of pure humbled power to those who come, because they know how powerful we are and what we offer them and the world. To be served by a priestess, to experience such a woman washing your feet, opens a man's heart even more to his beauty and respect. If a woman does this in our world today, most men will probably feel superior to her, not humbled. They would know they have power over her, and they would not even think of the fact that a goddess is to be honored and worshiped. I know... that's all-crazy mambo-jumbos talk in this day and age, where we have no idea what a woman truly is. Where women themselves have forgotten who they are.

But back then... I washed his feet with grace, with joy, excitement even, for we all felt this man was special but didn't know why.

I know the other sisters, all of us, are responsible for our fall, for believing his lies. I know that it is also no one's fault, but that little girl, hiding in the shadows, took all the blame as she sat there, for what felt like eternity, waiting to wake up from the nightmare she found herself in that night. From what felt like an endless trance of horror. She is the one who still holds this guilt and shame on her shoulders, and this is my attempt to make peace with her, as well as honoring the blood of our sisters.

God, why do people have to be so loud? With their freaking loud music from the clubs? I would get up to shut the window for some quiet, but my body forces me to stay on this chair, and the blood dripping between my legs whispers to me to keep going. My clenched hand is so heavy now it feels as if it is nailed to the desk. Something is birthing out of my body and there are no breaks now. I started this and I must finish, otherwise I know, it will consume me completely.

I'm kind of pissed off at that little girl and how naïve she was, but I also want to hold her and tell her it's not her fault. That she could never have known because she never experienced such pure evil. Because she was so safe in the walls of the Temple and the love of her sisters, enveloped in the sacredness of our way of living, that she could never have known as any of us what real evil looks like. And apparently, he can look like a tall, handsome piece of shit.

Yeah, and excuse me for my French, but even though I was a priestess once, or a girl initiated into being a priestess, in a magical realm of 3 moons and sacred daily rituals, I am more than that now. I am a fucking rageful woman that is not apologizing for her anger anymore. A woman who is now holding not only the pain of my sisters from the temple, but the pain and fear and trauma of all the generations of women since then. I hold it all in my womb. I always have.

Perhaps, if one of those dark, evil wizards is going to read this, know that you should have killed me that day, because just as he was the downfall of my world, I am here to be the downfall of yours. This world you have created with the wisdom and power of *our* blood. The world you keep distorting with the power of the blood of the children of the mother.

I promise you, your reign will end soon, even though I feel it will get darker before the light returns. It is women like me who will make you fall. No matter whether this is a tale or truth - *That* is a promise.

I don't know if it will happen in my lifetime. Probably not, but I don't care. I plant the seed on the sacred land of the mother and in the hearts of those who are ready to listen, and I promise, my words and the temple will return to guide the souls of sacred union once more.

And just to be clear, that man represents more than just himself. He represents the darkest cruelty of the deepest masculine shadow forces possible. And we all know what that feels like, sisters. You don't have to be spiritual or 'conscious' or 'awake' to know what I am speaking of. You have experienced this dark masculine force since the day you were born into this world.

I know these dark wizards are out there. They have been trying to get to me since I was a child in this life, especially since I began showing my face to the world. But they can never touch me in this life, just like then- I am protected. Untouchable. And they know it now.

They are out there. Perhaps they always will be, but you did not destroy all priestesses. And you did not destroy all the Sacred Knowledge that we hold. Because every single woman on this planet holds this knowledge within her. We all hold pieces of the highest wisdom, the same wisdom you took from us and used against us, and, personally, I will not stop using my voice, no matter how clenched my left arm is, to remind all my sisters who they really are, and, to remind that little girl that her voice is heard now, even if she had to remain silent as her sisters were burning.

CHAPTER 7

I remember the moment, after months of living in front of the gates of the temple, where he stepped his purified bare feet into the sacred Golden Gate of our temple. My big sister, P, and another sister both opened the gate for him to walk in and ritualistically, with a beautiful promising lie on his face, as he placed his hands on his heart, heard him reciting the powerful words that we have taught him. I don't remember the words, maybe because his smile distracted me too much to listen, but I remember the quiver in my body as soon as he stopped speaking. I was still a girl and not as wise as my older sisters, but I felt something was wrong in that moment and I'm sure that if I did, they must have as well. Perhaps he has gotten all of us under his spell, using our own powers against us. Using our own knowledge against us. What a beautiful lie he was.

I remember seeing my sister walking out of her room that day. I say it was her 'room' but really it was a Sacred Space, nothing like any room we have now, meant for sacred unions. Sacred sexual unions, I mean. And I knew she was there with him. I knew she would surrender her body and heart to him, but I was still blinded. So happy for her, feeling her pleasure and ravishment, thinking that she had created a true Sacred Union. The reason that we all do our work in the temple is for. But really, he was learning our ways, and she was teaching him... trusting him... he was manipulating her pure heart as she was open and surrendered as we all were. Trusting, powerful embodiment of the divine feminine herself.

She taught him everything. Even the things that were forbidden to teach most men.

... and some things that were forbidden to any man.

This is how much she trusted him; we all did. And I kept smiling and being happy for her. We all did, for it is our nature to celebrate our sister's sacred Union. Is our honor to do so. And we all offer our endless love and support to this path. Yes, this was unusual, but this man brought with him new ways, ideas and promises that spoke to our hearts. I believe my sisters, especially those who walked between worlds, were curious about his new ideas because they believed it would help them help even more worlds (dimensions and timelines).

Perhaps we have been so lost in our own ways of Divine Sisterhood and we have gotten too comfortable. I don't know for sure; this is just my own 40-year young idea of it, but really who I was back then and who we all were, is so much more beyond what my modern human mind can grasp. How the hell am I supposed to bring that kind of sacredness into a world that's so destroyed? While still knowing that the dark wizards are still out there just in different forms, still casting spells on us, just in different ways.

But I see right through them. I could always see through all the lies and deceptions, perhaps because back then I couldn't. Perhaps this is the gift of being born into a home of an abusive, absent father and a mother who is too loud. The gift of discerning. The gift of high sensitivity. I also know it is a gift that I am receiving from all my sisters.

... I need to catch my breath.

As I was fumbling my way naked, slipping over their blood, their precious blood that's been taken away forcefully from them, their blood and their power became my own. That heavy, thickening red mud transformed into the codes that penetrated my skin as I was crawling myself up into a scared little ball in that little nook in the temple. The only space I could find where all the candles had burned out, by wind or by fear, or simply because it was the time for their flame to be extinguished. Like ours.

At first, the blood terrified me. I felt their pain through it, but as the hours went by, in that corner of darkness, I allowed the blood to offer more of what it truly was. Information. Power. Courage. It became the Codes of memory I carried through lifetimes, like the heavy luggage I am so used to carry everywhere in this one.

I wore the blood of my sisters back then with so much fear and sadness, but I wear the memory of it now with honor and a courageous voice. Well, the sadness is still here... lingering in my veins, perhaps to remind me what is holy and what I love, and how much my sisters- loved me.

I will not just be the voice of my sisters who were slaughtered by an evil dark wizard and his alike, but I will be the voice of an entire world slaughtered. Of all the innocent animals, children, and people. I will be the voice of Truth, and despite the fact you may think I am crazy, I will be the voice of reason. An irony of my human existence.

I remember the ritual of the first blood. It is done when a girl receives her first blood. It is done under the moons, on healthy soil that is satiated with gold. A higher frequency gold than we have in this world now.

The Dark Wizards may have taken the memory of the mother from us. But they can never take the mother herself from us. We bleed her love and her pain each month. With the first blood, we invite the visions of the Divine Mother to fill the heart of this new Woman, and so, by bringing back this ritual to our girls today, we can, in a small yet powerful ways, return our spirit to the temple. We can reverse the magic back into light. We cannot rewind the clock, but we can recreate the power the temple offered us in our world again.

With our first blood, we each birth ourselves into a new world that we can choose. A reality we can create. We have simply forgotten.

The dark wizards have turned that beautiful, majestic world of the temple that I used to live in once, that was once my home, into a living hell. Using black magic, which was inverted Magic from the wisdom that we, the priestesses, have taught them, they managed to destroy an entire world and create a new one that was born from the ashes of a sacred world once burned.

You see, this world you live in now is ruled by dark wizards and by dark magic, as some of you may have heard me say before. And sure, you can think of me as a crazy lady or simply read this as a story, but as I said before, I am the Voice of Truth. No matter how it sounds to you. In fact, I know this truth will penetrate your mind deeper as a story, because this kind of evil is often difficult for humans to accept. Many times, until it's too late. It happened to my sisters and me. But never again.

What if all the fairytales were born of truth? What if all storylines told have a seed of reality in them? What is everything we know here is an inverted, manipulated truth, meant to blind you? Ask yourself, what if this story is ALL truth? What *would* it mean to you, your reality? And who would you be then? Who would you be called to become? For those of you who feel these questions and will have the courage to explore them, a new truth will emerge, a truth that might not only shake your world to its core, but your personal reality and the persona you have built yourself to play in it. So, I understand if some of you may choose to keep reading and not answer, and I also understand if some may choose to put this book down altogether, or even have the slight urge to burn it… either way, I will continue.

I will not let all that blood be used anymore by these dark Wizards. The only reason that they have had their powers is because they took it away from us, because they distorted it and manipulated it into their own gains.

But I am sitting here in this hotel in Bangkok. My hand is not clenched anymore, and I tell you, wizards - I am here and I am coming for you.

Every woman is a witch. Every woman holds the same codes I do. We have been burned at the stake in many endless ways by the dark masculine forces. In many generations, timelines, and societies, in many ways it had dictated for us. The wizards took away our wisdom but punished us for remembering and daring to use our own love and power. Took our voice because they feared it.

Hell, they even demonized the word witch. They distorted the idea of our inherent, natural womb wisdom.

Witch, priestess, goddess, woman. Whore. Mother. Sister.

"A woman's voice is so powerful that it had to be so subdued and suppressed by the dark masculine. For longer than history books can tell us, the female voice has been demonized by religion and male dominant society and labeled as evil, dangerous, stupid, possessed, crazy. The vocal cords in the female human body hold specific light. The codes of information that are stored in the womb. It is the frequency generator of the ancient knowledge and memories of who we truly are" – this was channeled by the sisters of the Temple, and I say –

I will not remain silent just because you are afraid of my voice. I will scream, sing, speak truth because those who walk their highest soul's path can hear it for what it is. They will hear the yearning in my cry, they will hear the truth in my anger. They will awaken in inspiration and new life with my song, which is the song of the Mother herself.

And as all my other sisters now awaken and remember who they are and come back to the temple, we will be unstoppable. And the blood that you took once forcefully is going to be shining brightly red all over this world- birthing, in Unified Bliss, freedom and true Sacred Sisterhood again- the new world of the mother. I say 'new' because we cannot go back to where we once were. We cannot go back to the days of the temple where everything was so pure and magical, but we can learn from our mistakes and we can create a world that is just as sacred and powerful and holds space for sacred unions, and yet is also wiser and can handle the darkness that you've introduced us to.

You see that little girl did not have to deal with such darkness. Not until that night the temple fell. But I do. And I know how to handle this darkness because I was forced to face it my entire life, my life back then, since that faithful night where the ground shook from the screams of my sisters, and my life now, with the human journey I have been on in a world born of darkness. Darkness that has tried to attack me in my dreams, in my visions. Darkness that knew who I was and has tried to plant fear in me my whole life. Darkness that is intelligent yet not wise. That seeks to destroy and torture the minds of all those who are like me, that here to birth light.

This darkness tried to scare me because I am untouchable, and now I know why I have been so protected my whole life.

Seeing demons, hearing the screams of animals in my head, and seeing the visions of children as they are raped and burned alive in hidden places. Facing this darkness has made me into a better priestess. A witch, if you will. A wise woman. A more powerful one that can transmute every shadow into light.

So, bring it on because our light will burn your darkness.

You are so weak that instead of worshiping the sacred blood between our legs; you had to cut it open from our heart with a knife. You are so weak that you had to take our wisdom and knowledge and, with endless resources of black magic, create your own new distorted world with it.

But because you are so weak, this lie of the world that you have created is also weak. And the only truth that remains is that I still hold a womb asshole, and that I still bleed sacred blood between my legs each month. And that I and all my sisters are the ones who truly hold the key to life itself. The key that you, long ago, took for yourself and tried to claim it.

Which brings me telling you of the true 'key of Solomon'.

Yeah, remember that King Solomon from the Bible, that was '*him*'.

CHAPTER 8

King fucking Solomon.

He wrote the new codes of demonic possessions. Books he gave to his disciples later that have evolved into the rituals many wizards still use today. We, the sisters, never wrote our wisdom down. It was carved on the walls of the temple and was held energetically within the walls, and the land itself kept the detailed records of all the codes passed down from a priestess to another. The air itself absorbed our love and moved it all around the earth, whispering sacred union knowledge to the hearts of all. It was kept with the upmost reverence and honor and transferred orally as well as through our wombs, but mostly it was kept and protected by the storytellers.

The storytellers were women who had one mission they deeply cherished – to form the wisdom and knowledge into stories which were told to each new generation of priestesses. These stories were told in such a way that each word held endless codes, each tale evoked memories of the wisdom within and every time a story was spoken, it pulled you into a whole new portal where you would be sure to be transformed. We didn't use the written word. Our voices, and especially the voices of the storytellers, which were encoded with specific hypnotizing powers of truth itself, were the force that kept birthing new life into the temple. Our voices. I remember their voices. And I only hope to have even a fracture of the power the storyteller's voice was as i tell you this tale now...

The memories of the sisters, of who I was, are kept safe in the heart of a mountain, where I, one day, would find it, in the future of that girl and the past of my 40-year self. I traveled to that mountain as I heard the call, climbed to the top of that mountain alone, reaching the snowy top. I wouldn't know, but my life had begun. As my own memories and the memories of my sisters de-coded back into who I am now. My body shivered on the top of that mountain, but it wasn't the cold. It was the memories and codes of the temple that found me once more. Or perhaps it was me who found my way back home again. I will not reveal the location of that mountain, for it will call you if you it must, and can you blame me for wishing to keep it safe now?

Solomon wrote the orders of blood magic that are taken by force. From animals, women, and children and by these codes, a whole new world and societies developed.

He was a dark wizard using our own powers and the knowledge that we had taught him - against us. He used his charms to penetrate our Temple, as well as my sister's body and heart, to learn all the true secrets that were once kept only to the priestesses of the Temple. Secrets of creating life itself, which he used to manipulate an entire planet with. To create an army of sadistic, evil men who think they can do better than us.

Well, I hope you're proud of your creation, because honestly sitting here in this Bangkok hotel room, I am not.

I am happy to inform you that my left hand is unclenched and relaxed. Night fell on Bangkok and I'm sitting in this hotel room in the dark, my body refusing to get up until I am done. The only light is from this computer screen, but my voice can see in the dark. I have gotten much practice. It is so clear and powerful; I feel as if a ton of bricks just melted away from my chest.

So, let's go back to talking about this Solomon dude, which was no King by the way. I stick to my story, describing him as the evil wizard he was.

A part of me really wants to say he had a small penis and was probably really bad in bed, but honestly, I cannot tell a lie, so I won't. I did hear the pleasurable sounds that came out of my big sister as he ravished her many nights in her sacred space.

Back to our story. So, Solomon stayed at the temple for many more months longer than most men do. We all accepted it because P created a powerful sacred Union with him and she was so happy, as he was being initiated to being a brother of the

Temple. He brought to my sisters great promises to even share the temple's love with lands across the world that still had some remanence of... well, disagreement. To be clear, I can't say 'war' because there were no wars in our world, but a few tribes did not live in the full ways of the mother, still had some fighting going on. At least, that's what Solomon had told us. Maybe that as well was a lie. We had traveled to many other worlds, but never to other parts of our land because we felt it, communicated with many across our earth and so we knew peace and harmony was alive. I am not sure how he was able to be so convincing. Such a masterful liar. How we all believed him so. I suppose we had no reason not to. We have dealt with many shadows in the other worlds, some more dangerous and deep than you can imagine, but perhaps we never thought we would have to deal with these shadows in our world. He was our brother. And we trusted them all with an absolute heart.

I also need to explain what a brother of the temple is at this point.

Those were men who gave their life as a service to us priestesses. They offered their lives to fully serve us in every we needed. Whether it is feeding us, taking care of the land and the temple itself, as well as serving our physical needs, in ANY way we needed it to be.

Aww, I wish I could describe in words just how worshiped we all were back then, how honored and loved by those brothers and by all men. And I wish I could describe to you just how much we loved and worshiped these men in return. But I can't. Because no words can describe that kind of devotion, honor, and love. That kind of deep respect and soul friendship. Not in this insane world the dark wizards have created for us.

Our brothers... I miss them, though their memory is faded after a lifetime of not knowing such power in men. It pains me, for I know the true beauty divine men hold. Such beauty, I am saddened to say, I still haven't seen in men of our time. I don't mean to sound depressing, and maybe it does indeed exist in a few men, but such magnificence, such power in their silence, their eyes... such safety in their laughter...and such ability to offer genuine pleasure...

What happened to the brothers of the temple, you may ask? Some were enslaved by the dark wizards, tortured to forget their purpose, pushed to oblivion away from who they were by pure cruelty. The dark masculine force spares no one. Some of my brothers were killed as they tried to help our sisters, and some chose to take their own lives along with us. None of these honorable men would ever choose to serve these demons, no matter what.

If you wonder about this idea of suicide, know that despite the religious idea that suicide is a bad thing, it is not. Every death is a suicide. The soul chooses how to leave the body, whether it is by accident, murder, or 'suicide'. The soul doesn't 'punish' you for choosing to take your own life. The soul simply is.

I used to see Solomon almost every day. I was mesmerized by his stories. Many of us were. The sisters that lived within the space that me and my big sister lived in (because the temple had many levels and spaces. It was a pyramid on the outside but there was also a pyramid facing down underneath the ground on the inside where we all lived and had vast halls, caverns, and spaces more magnificent than any human can build today. Some spaces where we performed specific rituals, ceremonies, and spaces where we gathered in teaching or celebrations.

No one else but the priestesses themselves was allowed within the lower pyramid. Only Solomon, that is... He found his way to enter that most sacred space somehow.

I want you to understand something before we continue. My sisters of the temple were extremely intelligent. More than I could express in our modern language. Their intelligence rose beyond logic and the written word. We were highly in tune to life around us. That was a part of what a priestess truly is. Being initiated as a priestess means you fully embody and live unified with everything around you and live, each breath, in that eternal sexual union with life itself, not just with one man. We held sacred codes and information for the entire planet, as well as other planets and dimensions - in our bodies, because of the state that we kept ourselves in. This is why we did not need to hold or keep our knowledge in a written book, but we transferred it through true initiation and memory of the sacred vessel (our bodies). One must fully offer her life to this path in order to hold such knowledge in the body, and we all did with joyful devotion, in each breath we took or gave to the cosmos all around us.

But this man, this beautiful lie that penetrated not just our body, but our entire planet's consciousness... He destroyed everything.

CHAPTER 9

For the same reasons that we should have kept him outside of the Temple, I will obviously not reveal any of the teachings and the sacred knowledge that he has misused. There are many of this generation who will use it again, in wrong, dishonorable ways, but I can tell you that this man offered us the idea to experiment with alternative forms of magic. He told us that he needs the power of the lower pyramid sacred space to perform this ritual and we agreed because we trusted him so much as he has relentlessly been serving the temple and the sisters for many moons now with such pure devotion.

I didn't really understand everything that they were talking about. I was still so young, and I had no knowledge of the high levels of initiation. Like I said, my blood didn't even come at that point yet. But I was constantly eager to learn. I remember following him around in the last few days as he prepared for the ritual. I didn't understand everything he was talking about, but the older sisters seem to be fascinated and open to his ideas. He promised the possibility of connecting with other worlds and helping them as well. Perhaps these were dimensions we have not yet reached ourselves. The priestesses destined for this path showed fascination and openness to his ideas. Those sisters had the abilities and responsibility to communicate with other dimensions. This is something that we have done already without his suggestion, for longer than time can tell.

One thing that the sisters have always done in the temple was to connect with other dimensions and bring the sacred knowledge of sacred union where it is needed- just the way they are doing right now by the way- through me- my human form, as well as my voice, my body and mind, which I gladly agreed to offer to them and the temple when they first contacted me on the 33rd year of this life. But that man promised something different. He promised what I could only understand, with my young mind and heart back then- the end of all suffering. He promised that we wouldn't even need to connect with other dimensions anymore because they will all live in the purity of the temple as we do. I don't really know what he promised beyond that. I'm sure there were many promises being made to too many of my sisters. He was a clever one, that cruel man.

I remember the day the ritual was made in the largest space of the lower pyramid, where we held the most powerful rituals to connect with other dimensions, as well as birthing New Life. Because yes, in the days of the temple, birthing a child was the most sacred ritual there is, and the mother was protected and safe within the temple, surrounded by the absolute purest of energy and codes. It was a space where only women were allowed. So, you can imagine the power and the energy that space held. In that space, life was being created abundantly and the blood of life that flowed freely as a sacred ritual filled each corner. This is the power that was alive there.

Power that he used.

Power that he harnessed.

Power that he manipulated to destroy us all.

I was not allowed in that space when the ritual was performed. In fact, I was asleep. So peaceful in my bed thinking I'll wake up the next day as I always do with a skip in my feet. But I felt the excitement of what was going on. We all did. The atmosphere in the temple the weeks and days before that ritual was intoxication. It grew larger as we grew in hopes and trust of him.

Well, by now you already know what came next and how I woke up... And what I woke up to.

The killing of my sisters took many nights. I was in hiding for a long time until I was found and brought to Solomon. He spared my life, but he took my world away from me. For some reason, he liked me and thought that I would be of use. He made me a slave of the other men. I was to show them the ways of the temple. To be their guide through the sacred walls, tunnels and caves which were filled once with utter magic.

Those men all morphed into one image of pure ugliness and monstrosity and this image haunted the deepest realms of my subconscious my entire life. I just never understood what it was until now. Each of them violated my body as they pleased, yet with a systematic, calculated coldness and all I could do was be silent. Too afraid to be as brave as my brothers and take my own life. Too weak to kill them all. The image that has haunted me is of a disgusting, twisted old man with a beard. His image is of all of them rolled into one in my imagination. I never understood my illogical fear and disgust of any religious man, but now I do. And they all look like those dark wizards because they have been their creations. Men who take, who hurt, who control, who destroy. Men who follow lies for eons, men who are weak, gross, ugly to their core. This is the image that has haunted me, but I feel now it slowly disappears and has no hold of me any longer.

As the days went by and the more blood spilled from my sister's bodies, a different kind of magic filled the walls of the temple. Not of the sacred blood of life, but another putrid potion of death. I could smell it. I could taste it. Reality around me became different. There were fewer colors all around, and my body could not float in the air any longer as it once did. The taste of food became more and more rotten and the air denser and heavier as the poison of their dark magic filled it, and as the pure, beautiful voices of my sister's song were replaced with cries.

The new priests came with their soldiers surrounding them and shattered the statue of the mother. Declaring this land as the land of their one God.

They prayed to their one God and cursed our sacred waters. With vicious, powerful spells we have never heard before, I saw the poison dripping out of their mouth, as their soldiers destroy the rest of the temple.

They did not dare rape and violate us, the priestesses. They knew our powers and that if they did so, it would be the end of them. In fact, he ordered them to never even think of engaging in sexual acts with us. Except me, of course. I was not yet initiated and was not powerful enough to influence them. I am glad that it was me who took all the pain, and they only had to feel the pain of the knife, and not the endless penetration of a monster.

They did, however, bring young, mostly virgin girls to the temple. I witnessed the violent rape of many, and for some also the violent murder and cruel use of their blood on our sacred altars.

I was helpless, but I used the little knowledge I had, trying to use some rituals and my will to send their souls into the womb of the mother and not whatever unknown, dark space he wanted to bind them to. Whatever force he wanted to sacrifice them for. Their bodies may have been mutilated, but not their souls. Their blood may have been used, but not their true power. In some horrific rituals those monsters cut out the wombs from the girls, and from some priestesses after death as well, but from the movement of the energy in the temple, I slowly realized they did not have the true knowledge of magic and didn't know how to use the womb. They thought they could, by the evil act of murder and cutting of the flesh, but what the dark wizards soon had to face, although they have not dared to admit this- is that they cannot use the womb. They cannot use the sacred blood; it is not theirs to use. It can only be used by women.

Solomon even tried to use the powers of some wise women, but they also could not harness the power of a dead womb - for the womb is even more powerful than any dark magic or will power of any dark wizard. This is, by the way, an important clear message, and a reminder of me telling this story. The power of the womb-man is hers alone. The wisdom of the temple belongs and is the right and responsibility of the priestesses! No man, no matter how knowledgeable, smart or strong he claims to be, cannot replace the womb. He will have to be born with a womb to do so.

The dark wizards who still carry on the 'legacy' of Solomon today have been endlessly trying to harness, use, and manipulate the womb in endless ways. Today also by programming humanity with the idea and ridiculous lie that there is no difference between a man and a woman. That even the word 'woman' is an insult. This will not last. It shall be the shame of this generation. We shall soon raise another new generation who will bring back the sacredness of the womb in a better way than before. A way that evolves with this age, in this moment in our evolution and those who will choose to continue with the lie of the dark wizards and be swept away with it, shall perish into a world as chaotic as they are. As selfish, cruel, and dangerous. We, the womb protectors, shall birth a new reality fit for those who wish to embody and hold the light codes of the temple once more. You don't have to know of the temple, or even connect to it. Most humans will not, they will simply naturally walk this path because they will be brave enough to hear the call of their soul. Of us. Of the sisters, of the mother. To return home.

Do not seek your answers to his-story in the bible. It is just another book. A book of tales, cursed with the strongest of magic, used as long-lasting propaganda for the legions... masses, followers. The names and circumstances changed within this book seen as the hollies one. Constantly altered with each generation of new leaders who needed a new storyline for their agenda that is more suitable for their time. The true history will only be found through the true awakening of the heart - ironically, what humans refer to as Christ consciousness. It is the only story that matters, the one that truly frees you, that awakens your soul, that calls you back home. The story we each awaken in our hearts. Do not let anyone dictate the truth to you. This is why the sisters have taught me to always offer the teachings and the knowledge of the temple AS a story. So, to give space to all who read it to connect to the temple and find their own truth. Not everyone's highest path IS to connect to the sex magic temple, but all can learn a thing or two and will gain inspiration of a sort from this 'story'. I invite you to Sovereignty. To sacred union on your own time, way, path.

A supreme irony is that religious leaders have been condemning magic while their (spell) book is filled with tales of magic, which they called 'miracles' of god. With stories of giants who are slayed by a small boy, of a staff that turns into a snake and of spirits speaking through fire or smoke... but that's not magic. No. that's just the force of 'god', isn't it?

It is not only magic that existed in the days of the temple before the dark masculine force took hold. The sisters were not only teachers and healers but could fly in their light bodies to any other dimension, world and connect to any timeline. To gain knowledge, to share knowledge, to help- when asked to, and to remind those who yearned for it- the true power of the sacred union.

There were all sorts of creatures walking this plane with humans, with us. What today you call fairies, elementals, magical creatures. The black magic of Solomon pushed them to run as well. Once the frequency lowered on this plane, those of the same frequency were forced to remain in a parallel dimension that is still connected to ours yet lessens in connection as we become denser and grow farther from our divinity. There was no more safe space for magic. For true freedom. That is when humanity actually lost its freedom.

When the temple fell, everyone did.

It is up to you to decide whether Solomon is a representation of this entire dark masculine world. This beautiful lie that we have been fed. It is up to you to decide whether what we call 'the Bible', that has been a book of high regards in the eyes of so many humans for eons, was in fact a made-up propaganda, disguised as a spiritual revelation that has been constantly manipulated with and changed according to their agenda, caging the minds and hearts of mankind. It is up to you to decide whether the Bible is in fact a spell book and perhaps it was created with the blood of all my sisters in order to give it so much power to manipulate an entire new world and generations to come. It is up to you to decide whether dark wizards exist or not. It is up to you to decide whether the temple was real or not. But I can assure you, for me, the temple was more real than any of the Bangkok air that I'm breathing now, than this wooden chair with a white towel on it that is soaked in my blood. The blood of my sisters feels more real to my body than any biblical story.

I can assure you as well that I can feel the pain of my sisters because we all share each other's pain through our wombs. So, if you have a womb, you can feel it too. It is your natural ability to connect to any other woman throughout time and space, though I can understand why so many women subconsciously chose to block this connection, because it comes with so many memories of so much pain and trauma. But whether we like it or not, it is our power and though it feels like a curse sometimes; it is what holds our true keys to freedom.

And in this dark world that the wizards have forced us to live in, our mothers don't teach us this basic truth. To feel with our womb, to celebrate our blood, to create sacred sisterhood.

Because our mothers forgot the powers of their own sacred blood as well. The power that flows freely between our legs each moon cycles. Blood that is in fact meant to flow for an entire life span of a woman but is cut short because we live in this toxic world that is, to say the least, an unsafe space to be a woman. A womb holder. A wise woman. A descendant of a priestess.

It is up to you to decide whether this story is real or not, but the undeniable truth is that those who hold the womb hold the power of life itself. And no matter what dark mind manipulations or new technologies you bring on us or how much you try to demonize, destroy, or manipulate our sexuality, this truth will never change.

This is why you, yes YOU- dark wizards, try to create new technologies that will replace the womb itself. This is why you try to make humans believe that there is no such thing as 'woman'. That sex is just a play, and that children and animals can, and should, be used as you please. And as the dark wizards continue in our modern day to destroy everything that is sacred within us - destroying the Sacred Union itself, destroying sexuality, destroying childhood, destroying motherhood and fatherhood, we will not stop holding the true Light-Codes of the Sacred Union.

We will proudly open our legs and allow our sacred blood to flow into the Earth with each moon. We will roar when we see our children being slaughtered and we will demand our freedom for pure pleasure and will express that in our own unique ways- because we all are the priestesses of the temple. We are the sisters you have killed and later, the witches you have burned and the girls you sold. You have built this world with our blood, and now we claim it back.

CHAPTER 10

You may wonder who the other men were. His weak, cruel disciples.

I do not wish to speak of those men who murdered my sisters. They have earned no space in this story or in any other. My sisters will live on through these words, but these men will continue being unknown. Their existence deteriorated like their hearts. Forgotten.

Unlike the true power of the goddess, that can never be forgotten. No, she only grows and expands no matter how many times you try to kill her, to distinguish her flame, for she IS life itself. But the shadow of darkness can be forgotten. And although their ancestors are now continuing to wreak havoc and create more chaos within humanity, the true children of the mother remember who they are and remember that the men of shadow have no true power. For true power lies within the womb and within truth. It lies within the hearts of women and men who serve the divine. Who seek freedom and sacred union.

When The followers of these men had no more priestesses to kill, they continued their killing of the witches, the midwives, the light walkers, the seers, and they did not spar the children as well, the holders of the power of imagination, which brings all life into matter. Harnessing All magic to themselves, these followers kept on bringing the stench of death and cruelty into this world and spreading it across the land that devolved into density. No one could float up in the air anymore. In fact, the mere idea was now a myth… but I could. We all could once, before the fall. In the world of the temple as I danced, I could float up, I would twirl with feet up in the air, painting golden rays as my movement brushed the ethers.

It may sound like a dream, but it was my reality. Our reality.

If it was a dream, it was soon to change as the dark wizards turn dreams into nightmares. And because they could not destroy the divine mother, for they came from her, they kept destroying her children and destroyed the memory of her from humankind.

But time is a circle. And we all knew that our time would return. As the ouroboros symbolizes to us, that all returns to where it began. The false gods have no light of their own. They needed the light of the mother in order to gain their power. But now, sisters, we are taking it back. Back into us, and through us, returning it to the mother.

I love to dance. I dance all my fears out of me. I dance all the fear out of all the children of the mother. Now, in this life and body, when I dance, I dance for you sisters. Be free through me. You still live in me and through me you tell your story. Our story.

No one can take away our freedom. Because here I am, a modern woman and a priestess of the Temple of once before, still alive, still speaking your codes and still dancing our power into life. I dance for the Mother, and she danced with me.

No one can claim the earth. No one can own the Mother. No one can control the feminine herself. Cage her. Place her in an idea. For she is everything and all and she is within everything and all. And all flows through her always, and all- returns back to her.

These men feared the power of the daughters of Lilith most of all. Lilith, the prime sister who lived among us, in many forms. Not in physical form, not etheric, but all. She who can never die was haunted for eons by men who saw her in her daughters. Killed them with swords, words, strikes of a hand, shame, guilt, submission.... but we live. These men forgot the basic truth, that without us, without the daughters of Lilith, they will not exist. Trying to destroy in endless ways she who gives birth to them, again and again. But Lilith whispers to us all a quiet roar only we can hear, womb sisters. We, who carry her flame in us forever. The prime source of our feminine human essence.

You come from us, men, and we hold your power always. This is a fact that the cold, fearful hearts of cowardly men can never accept. Their psych shackled in lies and terrified, knowing that true power will never be theirs. Trying to destroy now even the idea of 'woman' because SHE can never be destroyed.

Knowing the use of magic, the use of stories, they charged endless stories into one narrative with the blood of women and children. Taking the wisdom of the storytellers, they built a story that is a lie. That tells of Lilith, the 'demon' who will destroy all men. They learned how quickly the minds of men can be corrupted and manipulated. And they were right.

The dark wizards created a new generation, new people that we now call the 'chosen ones', but they were slaves. Followers of orders, weak in their connection to their own soul. People who chose to relinquish their power, their will, their choice, all to follow. To obey. They gave away all freedom for an idea designed to control them. They had forgotten the mother and formed the religion that would rule the world and inspire more of a sort. Legions of fearful, obedient people who will come to create new societies that sprung from the same fear. People who kill their own women, abuse their own children, who forgot what the sacred union is all about. They brought wars, hate, separation of lands, people, beliefs. Nothing that we knew in the days of the mother. Sacredness was lost when the priestesses replaced with male priests who made up new laws as they desired and used force and violence to those who disobeyed. They began punishing, in the name of their god of course- stoning, beating, torturing. Later, they burned the women alive. They called them witches, but their only crime was to live, somehow, in the ways of the sacred past. They remembered glimpses of the temple and lived, trying to remain connected to life, to nature, to the heart.

The priestesses serve the mother herself. For the sake of returning the memory of her to the hearts of all her children. They do not serve their own ego. True initiation shows who is a true daughter of the mother, a true servant of the temple, a priestess. Many today say they are teachers, especially of sacred sexuality, but they only serve their own ego. They pleasure others only for themselves, their false reputation and false information, but those who truly serve the mother serve to reduce suffering, to awaken humanity to their power. Sex becomes more than simple pleasure practice. It is for the sake of sacred union, and for that, a soul must be cleansed, ready, initiated. There are no shortcuts to true initiation. There are also few men who serve the mother truly and they are a blessing to this world. They usually work in silence, not needing to prove, to show off. They know the time of the goddess has returned and they support the women - their sisters who are here to teach, guide and show the path of the temple. These men are few, but their pure hearts are a beacon of light to us priestesses. You know who you are, brothers, and I honor you. We all do, here, in the temple.

CHAPTER 11

THE KEY OF SOLOMON

Many books were written by the next generations of Solomon's disciples in his name, or to honor his false name. Many manuscripts changed and altered with each new generation. Jewish kabbalists (magicians) and Arab magicians who were those who also created the 'religion' of Islam (which is based on the darkest parts of the word of Solomon, especially when it comes to harnessing the power of women, the womb by full control, fear, and domination. This 'religion', more than any other, works with very heightened demonic forces since the time of its creation and has brought much sorrow to this plane. The word of Solomon carried out and in time, new groups, 'religions and leaders began to spread. Some were forgotten, never to be captured in the books of history, and some are still having a hold of humanity today.

The key of Solomon is the most known of these spell books (including invocation and curses) who were written to honor Solomon.

It is divided into two books, and it is filled with clear spells for calling demons. What kabbalists today believe to be the 72 names of god are in fact derived from the 72 names of spirits that are explained in this book of spells. It is full of sigils, invocations, and blood sacrifice rituals of animals and virgins. The book was translated and changed many times, but we can see the ripples that Solomon had on generations to come as they keep the evolution of his dark, evil magic. Using the name of 'god' to evoke demons and calling Lilith an adversary. There is much confusion in the knowledge believed to be from Solomon, and it is for a reason. Darkness hides behind masks of light many times, using truths to tell lies and whispers evil while showing love. Darkness loves to confuse, to create illusions, because to its core, it has no truth.

Although many believe this book was written by Solomon to his son, Rehovham, only to be found by the worthy one who will read it and understand it. Solomon did write his words in a book and passed it on to the leader of his disciples for each next generation. His main focus was to find a way to eternal life so he could continue his legion forever, but he did not succeed. His demonic ways only brought him an early death, but he did manage to create a new world by destroying the sacred world of the mother as he destroyed the temple.

His objective was to summon, control and harness the power of demons and for that he used the blood of women, animals and in his last days, children. Although he failed, he formed a dedicated group of men who would follow in his footsteps, each with his own selfish desire to accomplish what Solomon didn't.

The lineage of these men still lives today, in what we call secret societies, passing on the distorted hate Solomon had.

The temple had a natural, white magic portal which he tried to use, and today these wizards still try in endless ways and with endless resources to create synthetic portals. The magic of the temple was powerful, but the black synthetic magic is weak and therefore needs so many resources to be sustained, and even still, cannot be as powerful as the temple.

The followers of Solomon and of such dark masculine type of forming magic believe the key of Solomon to be such a powerful manuscript of a complete guide to magical powers, but they are wrong. In order to bring this dimension to its glory and humanity to freedom, we must bring back our memories of natural magic, sacredness and unity. Magic that IS a sacred union with the divine. With life itself. A true, loving spirit will never demand blood to be taken from another. It will not have such rigid rules of ceremony. Only invitation for purity and sacredness that will help one return to their true nature. It will not force one to blindly follow rules made by fear and will call softly for one to walk into a path of self-love and power through soul initiation.

Just like his future disciples, Solomon conversed with low frequency spirits and received from them exact instruction to perform his magic, but he could never have done it without the sisters and the knowledge he got (and stole) from the temple.

According to the sisters, Solomon himself didn't use astrology, but his disciples did later after his death, when they kept moving from sacred temples to another, stealing knowledge. You must also understand that this all is not as linear as we think. Because these men, with the power of the temple, could now travel and communicate with other dimensions and timelines, they kept taking knowledge from many realms and use it to form their new world. The dark wizards of this time are attempting to do so as well, with technology and dark magic, but they are not as successful because they do not have the power and force that the first dark wizards had as they harnessed the power of the temple and the blood of the sisters. They had the most powers and even if you may believe that today's wizards may be powerful; they are not! They use illusions to make us believe they are! What do you think Hollywood is all about?

We used the circle in the temple. Its magic and power hold wisdom that exists beyond any time and space.

Solomon used it as well because he learned the power of it, but he also began using a sword, a tool the sisters never used. It was an act of violence to carve a circle on earth with a sword. Solomon himself didn't come up with this idea though, one of his men did, but it is still used today in rituals. The sisters explain that you can use a sword but never to cut the earth, only the air. Marking the earth can be done with a natural wooden stick only or one's finger. The magical sword is to never hurt anyone and to be blessed by sacred blood to give life, cutting the chords with anything or anyone that lives in the realm of lie, deception, or hate.

The act of cutting the umbilical cord also began with this black magic. The umbilical cord should never be cut between a child and a mother. It is to softly and naturally melt as the gentle process of the new soul to move from one realm to another happens.

We can use certain rituals and magical tools to transmute and change the intention the dark wizards formed for it. This is one example. The sisters also didn't use tools in magic. They used imagination which, in their light, high frequency realm, literally created and birthed visions, loving spirits and energies into life. They didn't have a leader in the circle- unlike what Solomon began in his days (him being the leader, of course). There were sisters all around the circle, and one in the middle who usually started the fire (that was usually in the middle of the circle with water around it). The dark wizards had no sacred blood, so Solomon used blood taken from them. Later, as the demons spoke to him more and more, as he descended into his soul's de-evolution more and more, they demanded more blood, more pain, more fear. This is how this world began to be inflicted by the black magic of such cruelty.

In the rituals where 4 women stood in a circle, they honored the 4 polarities- feminine and masculine, light and dark- to keep the balance. Which is what the sisters and other temples around the world always honored in their ways. To keep the balance of light and darkness and feminine and masculine. A balance broken by the dark wizards and their leader. In later timelines, where women remained honoring of the temple because they still knew it deep down and had a natural connection that kept the wisdom alive in them, they also used the 4 corners of the circle to celebrate seasons, which began to occur in this new world Solomon created. In the days of the Temple, seasons did not exist.

The prayer in the temple was always offered to the mother. As I began channeling the temple and translating its knowledge in this life, I was never spoken to by one woman who was the mother's direct channel. ALL the sisters, with their unique voices, brought the mother's voice into life. No one was above another. The dance they all created together helped the clear communication with the mother and the mother was felt and celebrated through their love. I asked in the beginning of my initiation for help to protect the Temple as I offer its knowledge. I asked to protect myself as I agreed to speak of this in public. I asked that only those who feel the call of the mother find my work and the Temple's wisdom. I have committed to keeping my voice as pure as possible. I gave my voice fully to the mother as well.

The men of Solomon had to form ways to protect themselves from demons because they opened the portals for them in the first place. They knew they could get hurt, so, while they were seeking new ways to use demons. They also had to protect themselves constantly from them and because we still live in the dimension they created, we do too now. Solomon brought this darkness from other realms because he had such darkness within himself, and he managed to poison many men as well. I say men because although today there are many women who worship demons and follow the baneful ways of black magic, then there were only men following Solomon. If only for the only reason that women were not allowed! The main reason Solomon even began his journey was to take the power from women, who were worshiped and honored above all because of the love, beauty, peace, and magic they brough this world. But he forgot, in his jealousy, that he is no woman. He is no womb holder and when a shadow of a man seeks to be worshiped; it is a recipe for disaster.

CHAPTER 12

Many works have been written under the influence of the sharp tongue and vicious mind of Solomon. Many works have even been written in his name. Throughout many generations to come, many men would try to imitate, use, and re-create his magic, which was not strong enough in its mystical sense. You see, Solomon was strong because he had something very simple. Manpower. He had a wicked verbal ability to poison the minds of men. He created the first re-legion army which killed the priestesses, destroyed the temple, and raped and murdered countless more, especially women and children.

The deep wound of women begins then, but the deep wound of men begins at that time as well, for they were not ready or equipped in that moment in time to protect themselves from Solomon and his men.

This may seem odd, illogical perhaps, because many of you are so used to understanding history in a certain form. A form that has been fed to you, but I wish to remind you that the dimension of the temple was a space of higher frequency and, as such, time did not rule the way it is now.

You must also inner-stand something about demons. Demons are tricksters. They always have been. One can summon demons, as Solomon did, but the true power demons have today is the fear one has of them. The illusion that one falls into when ruled by their own shadows.

I am about to state something that will anger many (again). The key of Solomon was a joke. A book rewritten many times by many men (a truth that very few are aware of) and which has tricked the minds of weak, gullible men.

Religion has been the primary tool by demons, and we can obviously see this (for those of us who have eyes and some logical mental capacity) in how each religion treats women, children, animals, and magic. We can see it in witch trials, in violent forced indoctrination, in the accumulation of wealth, lies, manipulation, raping of children, torture, and the use of black magic in plain sight while demonizing anyone else who dares use natural magic or live in the sacred ways of the mother.

I, the last priestess of the temple, am here by mocking you, weak men, of any timeline. Men who have been, and still are, using the most ridiculous, cruel forms of magic, repeating rituals created by weaker men before you, and seeking false powers of the lowest forms and spirits in existence. You, who have no self-power, no higher guidance of your soul, no higher purpose, loving vision, no care in your heart. You cannot create your own path but can only follow an already existing path, falling for any illusion, lie, and trickery known. You, who always find ways to cage the feminine, to harness and control the powers of all that is sacred, you- I mock. And I feel sorry for you.

Your churches will burn. This, I promise.

The irony is that Solomon himself would mock the dark wizards that have, throughout time, tried to live his work. Tried, and still try to master the art of black magic. You have no power, and never will. The portals you open are only charged with the power of life, of purity, of love, imagination, and the womb.

You use, you take, you lie, you destroy, and for what? You are nothing. You do not exist in the world of the mother, not until you choose to return to her womb, and return to your soul, which you have chosen to disconnect from.

This world gives respect to dark wizards, some knowingly, and some obliviously. It is we that must take back the power and consciously choose who we worship, respect, and listen to.

How tragic we have been so accustomed and deeply programmed to respect and worship false idols, teachers, leaders, while demonizing those who walk in truth.

The dark wizards have been cunning humanity with stories, ideas, and fear of the occult, which in fact, is not that occult. Magic is not hidden. It is all around. True magic IS you; it is me. It is in the air we breathe, and it is our birthright.

Do not be fooled any longer. Do not be blinded by their occult secrets that they wish you to believe you can never reach or truly understand. Their occult knowledge is a lie. True knowledge of the cosmos can be revealed to anyone who wishes to truly listen, to truly see and know and to purify their vessel (body) so they can actually receive light codes of truth. It is in the trees, in the land, in the air, fire and the waters of your body. It is in your shadows, as you bravely dive deeper to unite all parts of yourself that have been fragmented by manipulation. It is in sacred sex. In sacred union itself. YOU have the real power, and you always have.

I know very soon in our timeline humanity will see religion for what it really was this whole time- magic. Black magic. The dark wizards turned it into the idea of 'religion', selling a compelling story that manipulated the minds of men by fear and genius tactics of ruling the subconscious (true magicians KNOW how to control and manipulate the subconscious), in order to control humanity, to make them as well- slaves to the demons they serve and to feed these demons with life force.

The mother is the one who created earth, all life. But the dark wizard's idea of -'El' (literally means 'god' in Hebrew) took over this story of creation and twisted its meaning.

I want you to remember that I am using the simplest language here to explain this 'story', but your heart and spirit are the ones who will translate the truth for you, so keep them open and as pure as you can.

Why do you have to recite verses from the bible repeatedly? That is what you do with spells.

Why do religious rituals are so rigid and strict in every way? This is what ceremonial magic is.

Many Jewish religious people speak spells every day and don't even know it. They use spells written in the key of Solomon and have no idea they are conjuring demons. Or at least they are feeding them. Although the rituals have no power, the seed of them had and the continuous belief and life force people keep feeding them with does.

In a way, the temple was a gatekeeper. A protection for this world to keep the purity and high frequency of love. Jesus, whom by the way, was named a different name, knew this because his love and devotion belonged to the women who tried to keep the knowledge of the temple alive and the sacred union's wisdom kept safe. We call her Mary Magdalene. Jesus was a descendent of one brother of the temple. He still held the codes of the temple within him, in a time when darkness became too strong. His teachings included those of the sacred union but were deleted from the pages of his-story.

The rituals of the temple, filled with imagination, true natural magic, color, freedom of expression and pleasure that is connected to the pure heart space, are so different from the boring, rigid, colorless rituals that are done by the dark masculine energy. In divine feminine magic, you unite with the stars, with life, you experience the heights of extasy and love that cannot be described. And not to mention, it is fun! Because creation must be imbued not only with truth and sacredness, but with joy.

In dark masculine magic, you must follow someone else's rules, words and orders and the purpose is not to unite with life, with the stars, but to manipulate it, control it. I mean, if you are dealing with demons and inviting them over, you better know how to control them, otherwise, you are doomed.

Bathing is a ritual that Solomon learned in the temple and how vital it is. He never intended to unite with the water element. He wanted to dominate the waters and bind them to his will. But water cannot be dominated. You can curse water, but eventually you will end up drinking it yourself and curse yourself because all waters are one. Just like we all- are one.

Many names Jewish and Islamic people call their 'god' are in fact names of demons Solomon received with his encounters with them. He used to spend days and months in the main chambers of the temple, listening to the spirits teaching him and telling him exactly how and when to cut, kill, rape, and curse my sisters. I can see it clearly.

One of the horrific things he did was to make clothes. This may sound innocent, but the leather he used was from my sister's skin. Especially shoes. He began with animal skin, making cloaks for him and his men. This was the first time this had been done in my world and the sisters who were still alive and saw this with their own eyes... these are the screams I remember the most. Of my sisters as they hear the screams of the animals. These screams have tormented my day and night my whole life, and it is the fuel that keeps me going despite the challenges I've always faced.

Most didn't even wear shoes back then, but since the earth became a battlefield and men began to fight and run, they began to make shoes. The men wanted to make their shoes to be made from the skin of my sisters because this symbolizes the new lords of the land and their power over women, and especially over the priestesses.

Their absolute obsession with demonic entities became so morbid that later, in the next generations, the dark wizards began forming rituals of necromancy so they could keep communicating with Solomon himself and his first disciples.

Us sisters never called any spirit or demon. Why would we? When by serving the mother, we were able to live our most free, magnificent, unified lives and make sure all have the same privilege and gift of a sacred life. When we called the mother and communicated with her, we allowed ourselves to be vessels to what would appear to others today to be a 'channel'. But the mother has many aspects, many forms, faces, expressions, and we, her servants, allow her fullness to be lived through us. When Solomon saw this, he never understood it was the mother we let move through us. In his mind, all her many aspects were different entities. We merged with the mother. We devoted our lives to her, but he wanted to dominate and harness the powers of demons.

He learned all his wisdom from us. He took our power and distorted it into a new form of magic.

He- called many spirits and demons. We- just emptied ourselves to be her vessels of love. When the sisters were gone, her vessels too, slowly forgotten from the face of this earth, but, in another earth, my sisters still live. They are eternal, as the mother is, and she is more powerful than any black magic. It is simply the course this realm had to take, but we are still guided by the sisters and the temple, who seek to bring truth back to our hearts.

Just as we had the ability to connect to other dimensions, Solomon tried to do the same, but the only ones who could open these portals were us. Until today, the dark wizards are trying to do the same, and they have succeeded with their dark magic of sacrificial blood and technology. But we... We never needed anything but our love for the mother and the powers of the womb.

CHAPTER 13

Throughout timelines, Solomon received too much credit for things he was not and things he never did. As I mentioned in the book *Symbols of Sex Magic,* the seal of Solomon was named after him, although it is so much more ancient than him and he took its powers from the temple into this dimension.

As he could, for a short while, travel in time (in dimensions), thanks to the temple and the sisters, he had many wives as well as children who were never named in the pages of history. One of his wives, who thought she was the only one, was my sister. Their sacred union was a lie, which was the beginning of the descent of a world that would become one of false unions and dishonor of the sacredness of it as well as of the feminine.

My sister wanted to create a better world, like we all did. She even left with him for a while to his dimension but only returned to us a broken woman, discovering who her mate really was. There is so much more to this tale which I cannot share, for as I mentioned, time is not as linear for us as it is for you, and we could travel between timelines, as Solomon did, using our portals for a long time, during his time with us and the time after we were all gone. I am only sharing the important details which act as codes to awaken your own remembrance. Memories some of you may have, even if you never even set foot within the temple itself. For you see, dear ones, although the temple was my home, the temple is also- forever within you. My sisters and brothers. We have the ability to transform the power of the sacred symbols, the sacred union, back to its original form, while maintaining the codes that fit THIS timeline. For each timeline, each epoch, each generation has its own unique codes. Although we cannot live as the sisters lived in the temple, we can use their wisdom to bring the knowledge forth to this moment in the best way to serve our evolution.

In the time of Solomon's rising, there was a need to evoke and protect from demons, but now, in this era, those demons do not exist. What people foolishly still try to evoke are low spirits that are disguised as demons. The black magic of Solomon literally has no more room in this reality and time and those who still walk in his path are foolish and only cause chaos in their own soul's evolution as well as humanity's.

There are many changes occurring now in the spiritual development of humanity as we move to a new age. The old ways no longer serve us. The sisters wish to be clear that they do not wish for us to copy their ways. They have lived in a completely different space: frequency, density, and reality. What they wish to do by channeling their wisdom now is to give us the codes to elevate our souls in our time. My (very challenging) work has been to not only channel this knowledge but 'translate' it into our era, so we can use it in this modern age.

In the past, the idea of a 'guru' was prevalent, but now, the guru is within. The system that fits us now as we evolve, is the pureness of oneself so that you can be your own guru. For this, we need true initiation and to develop this power from within. This is why, despite many requests, I do not like to teach classes because I am only here to be a messenger, and as such, I must be in my own constant initiation and always keep my vessel as pure as possible. This is the feminine time. The sacred feminine that calls us into our soul's adulthood, spiritual maturity, and responsibility.

In this new age, death is no longer the fear that guides us. As we embrace and honor the feminine once more, we embrace death itself as a magnificent gift of life, and we are no longer ruled by the fear of death/ subconsciousness/ the black sun/ the feminine.

When we fear the feminine, we fear life as well, and we live as shells. As empty vessels and disconnected channels to the afterlife, to the cosmos. This is what the dark masculine energy has done to us, and we see it with the programming of the deep fear of death that every religion has given to humanity. This fear creates a regression in our evolution. This is the true 'anti-christ' impulse we all have shared as humanity (ironically, while following the idea of a 'Christ').

This reversal is pure black magic in plain sight, which we have been under its spell for thousands of years. But no more. The coming of the sisters to this realm with this knowledge is the greatest sign we are moving from this shadow.

Solomon believed that the power of the sisters to travel in time, to create portals, comes from external technology. The same technology that his followers still try to create until this day. But true 'technology' is that of the womb. Is that of the natural soul of the mother embodied fully within the wombs of the sisters, women, who are brave and loving to the point of utter surrender to life itself.

True power never came from an external source, only from within. This is the correct meaning of the christ consciousness that has been manipulated by Solomon's lingering energy that has passed on and got empowered yet distorted through each generation of his men.

They took the truth and reversed it into a lie. They used anything sacred and powerful and harnessed its life force.

Just as the power of life is through the internal process of the womb. Of taking the seed IN, allowing it to transform you from within, and only after- give life. We cannot create life without. As well as true evolution and initiation.

The horrific black magic we see that is pushed today, of creating an artificial womb amongst others, will destroy humanity to its core, for it is NOT the way of materializing. It is an illusion of materialization that has no spirit. No connection to source.

Without the feminine, there is no source. All comes from her.

This is pure inversion magic that brings forth an undeveloped illusion of life. Of creation. It is a creation without initiation, and therefore it is empty. True initiation begins and ends within.

This descension brings the fall into pure matter. Into the illusion of creation with no real creation and especially, no real evolution.

AI, genetic modification, artificial intelligence, and artificial wombs. All combined with black magic, with the same black magic that Solomon began sharing with all his men and sons, in many timelines.

NOTE (from *Symbols of Sex Magic*): Solomon is just a name. The sisters of the temple explain to me that the name of the man who did this dark magic was named differently in their reality, but they do not wish to speak his name at all because the powers he had created, as well as his essence, is well to be forgotten. Solomon is the name he used to keep his memory alive in the pages of the written his-tory he began. His magical name he used for himself and that other used for him. Any good witch and wizard know that the choosing of a name is one of the initial steps of initiation.

When men try to play God, they only sign up to a one-way road of de-evolution. They destroy themselves. They will eventually reach a point where they are no longer human and will remain fragments of who they were, as well as reach a point where they will no longer survive and will need to begin their cycle all over again. How ironic it is that the fear of death will bring to the real, final death of a soul. The only way of evolution and soul growth is by loving death, the constant change of the feminine and embracing the womb, the source itself, the sacred union and true initiation — that comes- from within.

Trauma has trapped us in time. As individuals and as the collective.

The leaders of this age still try to hold on to dear life to the last age. This also creates devolution. It regresses us backwards, but some of us who have fully healed trauma can be in this full present time and its correct initiation. We can bring forth the correct pattern that will evolve us NOW.

With each age, the planets change, the tools change, the codes change. We must purify and heal and ground in this timeline so we can move forward organically, guided by our inner soul and source itself (which I call the mother).

Now, as we are preparing for the next level of evolution, we must embrace something new, and we also must let something go. The latter is extremely challenging and even life threatening to those who cannot let go of the old age. Especially those who follow (consciously or not) the old ways that began with Solomon and the birth of the dark masculine force in our realm.

We cannot use old magic that does not fit this timeline and expect change. We must fully embody the correct codes of the feminine, the masculine and the sacred union that fit this timeline, and for this, we must be initiated. And in order to be initiated, we must fully live in the heart and purify it to hold the purest of love.

So many today still use magical rituals, ceremonial magic and rites that have no hold in this dimension and timeline any longer, only keeping them in a de-evolution. This is the time of the mother, the pure love and initiation from within. This is not the time to follow someone else's rules, rituals, and ideas.

If we do not understand the time we are in now and the codes necessary for organic evolution, we will allow our soul to fade. Eating animals is one of the more prevalent black magic rituals that has no more space in this world and anyone still choosing to participate in this practice daily is literally on a soul de-evolutionary path.

It is time to birth new traditions that will assist the development of THIS TIME.

These will only come from the sacred union itself and the path of true soul initiation.

Many old traditions, like Hinduism and kabbala, have some truths and wisdom, but they were only suitable for a specific time. We must evolve now. The new traditions slowly birthed now are clearer and more precise. They have no need for allegories or confusing patterns that leave room for confusion, chaos, or insertion of lies or distortion. These new traditions that are now born of the sacred union will not leave out the feminine, for they are divine feminine in nature and as such- hold within them ALL- the feminine *and* the masculine, for the feminine, as opposed to the masculine - is all-inclusive.

Solomon's magic was not internal. This is why he had to summon demons. Entities. This external black magic was going on until now, but now is NOT the time anymore to summon, to call in, to ask or beg for salvation from any external force. Now that we are at a time of healing and transmuting, we have arrived at the gates of inner alchemy and wisdom. Any true path will demand purity and cleansing - of body, mind, heart, and soul, because if one is not purified, true initiation as well as true receiving of codes and wisdom cannot occur and it can even damage the individual. So, if you are trying to create sacred union or simply to evolve as a human but still consume animals you will cause damage not only to the animal, but to your soul, body and evolution. There is nothing sacred about this black magic ritual we all have been taking for granted as a way of life. Let us evolve.

You cannot speak of love and unity and cause suffering and separation from your daily actions, words, and decisions. This is misaligned and will bring chaos into your reality in many ways. This connects one with the lowest entities and dimensions possible. The effects on humans are unfathomable.

Solomon has opened the floodgates to lower vibrational entities that still walk this realm now, although the same demons he had summoned cannot be summoned any longer. Again- because of the time and density we live in as opposed to his time and density.

As now we mature, purify, and grow, many of us slowly become independent of external entities and can slowly discern better from truth and deception.

This should be a reassurance to you, light humans. That those who still seemingly hold power on your planet, have no real power. They still need to summon entities to gain power, or to feel they gain power. What keeps them in power is not that they have power - it is that they managed to fool humanity that they do. They do not have powerful demons helping them, but low frequency entities that are stuck in the 8th sphere. The cesspool dimension where all collective shadows and lowest frequencies accumulate in. These entities still can and do affect humans and influence our world, but the more you keep yourself at a higher frequency, the more LIGHT you literally become, the less they can match to your dimension, and you become untouchable. This is not about protecting yourself, it is about keeping your heart and vessel (physical body) as clear, purified, and connected to source as possible. And there is NO way you can achieve that by consuming animals or having unconscious sex with others. This cannot happen if you fill your body with vaccines, medications, alcohol, ego driven drugs and hate or any desire to hurt another.

You must live in a symbiotic relationship with life itself as you walk your path, knowing you are a part of all, and all is a part of you.

At this time, we do not need demons, angels, or gurus. We need ourselves. Our true self is to be reborn from the shadows of our own trauma, to unite all our fragmented parts from all time and space into oneness. We need the alchemy of inner union.

This is the time of inner alchemy of the heart, which is the only 'guru', spirit, or 'god' we need. It is the time of pure spiritual independence and freedom. Go within. Be within. Birth from within.

When it comes to ISIS and LILITH, who speak to me as well as the sisters of the temple, I want to be clear. Yes, they teach me. They speak to me. But I am equal to them. They are not here to save us, just as I am not here to save any of you. They connect with us to remind us of who we are. To offer us a path to our own power. Even ISIS never actually speaks to humanity. Though many think she speaks to them and looks to her to rescue them. She is a code to remind us of our own power. LILITH is the one who usually speaks to women and men currently, but she never actually lingers. She awakens YOUR OWN POWER for you and will not let you lean on her for power. To those who evoke her in such ways, they are not communicating with her, but an illusion of a lower entity, so beware when evoking LILITH. Give her the honor she deserves and be wise. She will not honor those who still practice any form of black magic (including animal sacrifice and consumption). She will never ask for anything in return for power. She will not stay with you forever and will give you all the answers. She wishes you to keep questioning everything and to rise into your light.

THE OLD SEALS AND MAGIC

The old seals and Solomonic magic do not fit this time any longer. We have shifted, especially since 2016, when the sisters first created an initial contact. They did so because it was the proper time for us as humanity and I feel I just happened to be the best candidate at that time, due to where I was on my own personal journey, my self-initiation and especially my high levels of integrity and sense of justice that is crucial for this task of translating the codes for humanity at this time. I was by no means the only one suited for this task at that time, but the sisters also tell me that other variables have been taken for account and one of them is the future timeline of each candidate and whether it will be beneficial for them to still be the best in service of the temple for the long run.

The only seal - sigil- symbol that will still be appropriate for ages to come is what we know as the star of David, though the sisters ask and hope that we no longer refer to it as such. The new generation will have a new name for this symbol that will be the best for its power for the next age, but for now, I will refer to it as Kohav or - meaning 'star of light' in Hebrew.

CHAPTER 14

We are even now.

Me and that little girl.

I will get out of this chair in a few minutes and perhaps go grab something to eat as I know that she is running naked and free in the Temple, with all her sisters again, alive by her side. Because perhaps just as the world of the temple could reach our dimension and communicate with us, I can communicate with them now and say- beware of that man who is tall and charming, a man so many one day will mistake for a king. A man who will offer new promises and ask to enter the sacred hall of birth. Perhaps I can reach out to you, sisters, wherever you are, whenever you are, and call to you with a silent roar to keep to your sacred rites no matter what promises any man will give you. Perhaps they could hear me now and perhaps my big sister, P, will not allow that man into the temple at all, and into her own temple.

Because, after all, if we are honest, we all have a Solomon, or have dealt with our own Solomon in one shape or form. We all saw, felt, and experienced the shadow masculine in our life as a woman. We all fell under a spell of one who wanted to take instead of giving, as the divine masculine does. We all know or knew at one moment in time, a Solomon, or some form of him. A few of us may have fallen so deep because of him that we had to fully die to re-emerge as a new version of ourselves. We all also know or wish to know a man that embodies the love of the brave temple brothers who worship and serve our highest form of the mother within. This is what I invite your inner sex priestess to evoke, to call, to nurture and to love. This devotion and honor are the only gifts we must except from any man, but we must first embody it.

Perhaps I could whisper into the ears of that little girl I once was, telling her the truth of who he really is, telling her to speak up and use her little voice. To say when something feels wrong. I wonder what would happen to our world, what would happen to this modern-day Bangkok version of me?

Would this story ever be told? Would it even need to be? I leave it up to you.

PART 3

THE SISTERS

ENERGY AND LIFE CYCLES

All matter is energy, and nothing can be destroyed or created. The mother has already birthed all energy from her womb. In that force, we humans named 'the big bang', which no man can ever truly analyze, explain, or find rational scientific proof of. She already released all matter from her eternal orgasm, which we are the living ripples of. There is no death and no end. It is all a cycle. Life can only be transformed, so it never truly ends. We are, though, in this physical reality remain with the karma and karmic debt we create and will suffer the consequences of all we choose.

We also believe some things live and some are animate. But the sisters also know that all is alive. That all is a part of the same magnificent force born from the womb of the mother. Knowing this and embodying this truth, the sisters are at peace. They have also transmuted their pain and trauma by now to a new life. A new reality. The same reality they are communicating with us from now.

The sisters are like the phoenix, rising again and again from the ashes. They are eternal for their life force, energy and magic is eternal and will always have space and a reason for existence in the world of the mother. In any time, space, or reality. They will also eventually, as they do now, will find their way to any dimension.

What we must understand in this reality we live in now is that there is the law of cause and effect and that we are also heading to a space where no life that is not fully symbiotic to all other lives will cease to exist. This goes for humans (who kill animals, burn, and rape and destroy everything else thinking they are superior) but also for animals who consume other animals (which are only doing so because of their connection to human evolution and mirror a state of our consciousness), as well as plants, viruses and any other form of life that do not live symbiotically with all other life forms.

This part of the cycle has already begun and those alive now and, in the generations to come are the seeds of this shift that are inevitable.

There is no time of creation or destruction, although to us it will definitely appear to be so, many times over generations, until we fully (hopefully we will) come to a place of living in this symbiotic harmony with all life. We are planting the seeds of change. Right now. Each of us with the choices we make, the intentions and integrity we choose at each moment.

I am not in my hotel room anymore. I am now waiting for a flight back home. What I have decided to call home for now-California.

I know my time to ground, to nest, to rest has come. After 20 years of wander. I may not be a gypsy for a while. I may not carry heavy luggage around for a bit, but I will keep traveling and living in many worlds, as I always do. I am a priestess of the temple, and I live there with my sisters, completing the initiation that was taken from me once, but I do so while I am also a priestess of this new era. I know I will keep seeing the visions of children being tortured, and I will keep hearing the screams of animals being slaughtered, but now I have new powers, as I know I am home and always have been. Now, I know how to turn the screams into roars and transmute the cries into fuel. Held, loved, and protected by the Temple and my sisters, as they initiate me into my greatest version, and as I help the initiation of more sisters.

In this world that has lost its magic, I live a magical life because of the fact I have given my life as an offering to the mother herself, to truth. Just as I did long ago, thanks to the woman who birthed me, who knew who I was even before I emerged from her magnificent womb.

THE SISTERS SPEAK:

The abuse of sexuality will reach a point soon where the dark forces cannot hide anymore. This will be the peak point where the fall will happen. The fall of mankind's consciousness and with it- true freedom.

Just as in the last days of the temple, this point is near, though the use of children in dark sexual rituals have been prevalent since the days of the fall of the temple, humanity is nearing a point where the darkness will seem to take over completely. Where the use of innocent children will no longer be hidden or shameful, but an accepted part of your society. Some people will call it 'natural', and even say this is an expression of 'love'.

Beware of these signs and prepare yourself to leave this falling dimension. Just as we, the sisters, have left our dimension before its fall.

Those of us who were not murdered, escaped, and reached a higher frequency world where we can keep our wisdom alive and safe. This is also why we can communicate with you now, through this time and space. With the love of the mother, we as well, birthed a new dimension into existence. The true temple can never truly be destroyed.

We urge you to prepare your vessel, your physical vehicle, as well as your heart and mind for this ascension. As Luna always speaks, the most important thing for the vehicle is your diet and what you consume, but to eat light, plant-based foods is not enough. Honoring your shadows, your ego, as you call it, and taking responsibility, living kindly with one another, and reducing any suffering you may cause any other life, as well as the planet itself, is vital. Activating the heart space and honoring your sexual life force.

Above all- Taking the true path to sacred union.

The fall is near once more, and it has happened many times before in humanity's repeating cycle of evolution. Each time, the immoral and distorted ways of sexuality and dark magic lead the path for this to occur. This is one reason that the story narrative of 'light vs. dark' and of magic is always so prevalent in your collective psyche and seems to be so seductive to the minds of so many. Magic is who you are. It is in your nature, not just in ours. It is your birthright and always has been. A part of the codes of your DNA, which science will one day discover in the next 3 generations (for this timeline we are speaking to).

Those of you who see the truth behind the lie and the illusion and dare to speak of it are considered crazy at this time, and even shamed for their opinion and knowledge.

Many of you follow false magic paths and teachers. Many of you have not found the ability to see truth, not because you are unable to, but because you chose to remain in your own shadows that feel known and offer false safety. We hope that many of you will soon return to the ways of truth, of honor, of initiation. That you will return to the Mother, for when we are back in source, in the womb, our sight is clearest.

Prepare for the fall to happen and stand your ground. Know when to speak your truth and when it is futile to do so and preserve your energy, directing it to raise your frequency in preparation for the ascension- as many of you call it. (We try to use language that is simple for most to understand and mostly to feel).

Your 'health' organizations begin to release different 'potions' (which are scientific substances that are injected with dark magic. Yes, this is real and happening for years now on your planet), that prevent your children from not only expending their physical vessel and have a clear path to their own evolution to contain their highest form of masculinity/ femininity, but also, these injections and poisons in the food and drugs, will prevent the natural connection to their higher self. You must protect your children, ALL children. Even if you have none of your own, know all children are yours, for this will affect you directly, as well as your generations to come.

We regret to say this, but we must prepare you.

The dark forces have been preparing for this age for eons. Since Solomon the king took over the temple and the rites of sacred union, this path has begun.

The rise of their 'beast', as some call this force, which is really a combination of many low vibrations, demonic entities that the dark wizards have been opening portals for on your planet since then, is inevitable.

This WILL happen on this timeline if you are reading this.

Please DO NOT FEAR. We can assure you that this knowledge will only set you free- we guarantee - if you take the correct steps now and CHOOSE your highest path.

Prepare.

In order for the demonic forces to fully enter your world, humanity must be lowered to a state low enough to match their frequency. To be in a state of mind so distorted, confused, and immoral as well as sick- on all levels of the psyche - to accept those shadow forces.

For those who awaken in this age, these dark times ahead can be a powerful rising into your power, as the warriors of light you are (again, we use words that will provoke a memory in most).

Many will remain on this timeline, seeing the shadow and lies, but will not fall for them, instead they will bring the new light codes into this reality. Helping human evolution and balancing the scales.

They will watch the enslavement and torture of many. They will bravely stand on the battlegrounds of demons and masters. They will strive to keep the natural ways in a world that revers material gains above all. They will witness a world of overly medicated, mind controlled, sexually lost generations who are disconnected from all that is sacred and natural, as the programs get deeply more distorted through education, media, new ideas of 'free' love, relationships and of course, sex. For you, we wish to remind you- this will not last. Remain the rays of light you are and as you leave this life, know you have kept the light steady here with your love. Also know (this is vital for you to know) that your soul can now choose any future timeline, world, life and experience you wish. YOU can always choose what life you are going to after this one.

The spirit of humanity will be enslaved by their bodies.

The demonic forces will not rule for long, but the fall will be a devastating one for humanity. It will bring to a death of the spirit in order to call on a new re-birth of humanity's collective soul. A sort of enforced maturity, if you will, since the point has come when this maturity was not achieved by choice.

The complete destruction will inevitably call for harmony and union of humanity's fragmented, traumatized parts. To come together again, and after a time of healing- birth a new generation of new, evolved souls.

This will take many generations because the DNA as well as the spirit and collective trauma of humanity must heal and be transmuted into something new. Eventually, technology will seem to 'fall' again, and take on a new form of use by humans, as they find their path to nature again, in a new, more balanced way. This book will be found by those who walk the path of high evolution in every next generation and is meant as a coded reminder of their soul's courageous path. We love you.

The last 60 years or so have been the greatest for the dark wizards in their preparation for their lords (demonic forces) to enter this realm.

World war 2 of your world was one of the biggest portals opened, but they still did not have the proper technology that can be combined with the knowledge of dark rituals they have kept developing. They knew what it was, but only today they have the ways to implement it, though they have expanded their plans as time went by and came up with crueler and more sophisticated ways to manipulate mankind.

Their plan is at a peak and has reached a new peak with the new 'virus' era you all recently experienced, which we will not get into here and now.

The main force they seek to call in (they call it 'baal'/ Ahriman, but also other names they use in secret to summon this force), is planned to be alive in a human form, as a public figure. They have tried before, but full hosting of this force within one human body was not yet successful (in the year of 2023 when we speak these words to you).

This demonic force (which again, are many demons formed into one force), uses many symbols to program its codes in humanity's subconscious mind. As we have taught Luna Ora, and as some on your planet already know and have been trying to share this knowledge as well, we ask you to notice the symbols. Learn about them, master the knowledge of the subconscious mind, because for those of you who will remain here as the warriors of light, they will be useful, as you can invert them back into their original form and use their power against the wizards. This will require a pure vessel. Also, when one has mastered their subconscious mind, others cannot manipulate it and use it against them.

We also wish to mention that, for some of you, the word 'wizards' may be too 'fantastical' for your mind to accept. That is perfectly fine. Honor your own belief system and use a different word if that suits you. We use that word because that is exactly what these people are.

At this time (your year of 2023), you are heading towards the darkest of times. But we ask you to remain in your own high frequency, no matter what the narrative fed to you from the external world may be.

Feed your own mind and heart. Connect more to each other and nature. Live in the purest compassion for any plant, tree, animal, human, and yourselves. Connect to the mother once more, who is source itself.

As taught in our initiation, to see her with the eyes of a priestess is to see her as the eternal Womb we all come from and return to. And again, if the word 'mother' doesn't suit your belief system, change it, but we recommend not to call it 'god', or any other masculine word, because it will assist your evolution in the best way at this time. You must transmute the ways of the dark masculine energy and connect once more to true source, a source that holds both divine masculine and feminine- which, in its best, highest symbolic (and literal) form- and this source IS- the mother.

Your earth is going through its own inner 'battle' as you are. Its own evolution, and it will show you the chaotic waves created by the opening of these portals by the wizards. Weather will act differently (you are already seeing evidence of this each day). It will be more unexpected than ever before. Especially floods, which will be more prominent, and more humans will die of illnesses, or 'natural' disasters. Temperatures will be unexpected and surprising in many parts of the planet; many species of animals will die and many new ones that hold new codes and frequencies needed for this time—will emerge from what it seems- nowhere.

This is the gift that animals are for humanity, by the way. It is time humans understood this once and for all. They hold specific codes, information, and frequencies that humanity cannot survive and thrive without. When humans destroy and hurt animals they quite literally- hurt and destroy themselves. Even if this doesn't make 'sense' to you, we ask you to feel this in a deep space within your spirit and heart.

The 'beast' will rule. It is inevitable at this point on your timeline. The good news is that it will not last long. Most of you will witness the fall of the beast as well, though the shock waves of his presence will echo for a few generations to come and they will have to 'clean up the mess', as you say. This is the 'bad news', as you say.

This is what the sisters have to say, and now, allow me a moment to share my own thoughts.

I am grateful for their information as they prepare us. I can't say I am surprised, though I did not know all these details.

I have had dreams of floods for years now. And now, as I write this book, I am being called, after 20 years of living as a gypsy, moving from one place to another on this planet, to find a home. And there is no doubt in the call I hear now to be far from the ocean and find a home in the mountains. This is the loud call I've been hearing for a while (though I've been trying to pretend I do not). I traveled to the beaches of Thailand this year, hoping to enjoy the peaceful life on the island, but was forced, time and time again, to leave the islands. I kept moving for the last 4 months, and each time my plans were interrupted, I lost so much money and had to, not by choice, again and again, to change direction. It took me months, lots of energy and money to finally accept the fact that I must prepare myself. To find a safe home. To nest. And as someone who has traveled for so long, I tell you; the world is changing. Flying to different places is more difficult, the control, laws and regulations shift rapidly, and censorship is tighter. Like so many, I am not allowed to speak as I please on social media and for those of you who watch my videos; I have been under an attack on all platforms.

But I will not stop. Truth is our only hope.

We simply must find new ways to share it.

I have much more knowledge of sex magic from the temple to share with humanity. I share it as the sisters guide me, when humanity is ready to receive it, and as I- the channel- also ready to hold, embody, and share in the best way possible.

I am always deepening my own initiation, as I have given my all to the temple in this life. Just as I did before. And if needed, will do it all again.

THE SISTERS CONTINUE

The planet, the body of the mother (one of her bodies) is on a journey to restore its consciousness, as humanity is. It is not an easy journey to make, as the dark forces push against this in every way possible.

An awakening from a deep, long dream is happening to humanity and the planet now.

The pyramids of your timeline, known as Egypt and south America, have been used for high black magic. Many of you believe these pyramids were a place of powers to be revered, but we assure you they are not. Their image, as well as magic, has been, along with much of your history, manipulated and changed to benefit the dark wizard's plan.

Beware of the knowledge that claims to be of your ancient Egypt. Also, if you choose to visit these pyramids, you must learn how to do so and place a powerful protection around you. This does not mean that Egypt has no powers. On the contrary. The lands of the middle east hold immense powers. That is why they have been taken over and a long-lasting play of war has been directed by some. The codes of those lands will soon be able to be set free. This is all we will share at this moment.

Expect many floods and draughts in many places in the world. As the waters of the mother transmute, so will the waters in each of you.

Many portals have been tried to be forced open.

Many events happening that are not reported and kept hidden from humans.

Much is told to you in the form of 'stories' in your media, books, films and music industry through many forms of art (and symbols).

New lands have and will continue to appear, although they are kept secret.

New creatures appear, although kept secret (for now).

Many of you will be communicated by these creatures. Some of them will be what you call- dragons. They may appear in different ways. If you get connected by one, listen. Do not fear. Open your heart and allow them to guide you. Make sure to always say "only those of the highest form of love and light are welcome here.", because some demons will disguise as higher beings and guides. If your body is still tainted by the dark forces of animal products, you will not be connected by real dragons- if that happens, it is most likely a demonic energy in disguise.

Higher beings with such pure light cannot communicate with a vessel of lower frequency, such as one who consumes the flesh and blood, or any bodily fluids of another being. It is simply not possible. You will attract the frequency your body and heart are in. So, beware and be wise.

Inner earth is not a myth. It is a place sought after by many of your earth's leaders and has been the cause of many wars, though this was not known to humanity. It is a realm outside of this dimension, though. It cannot be reached by simply digging a route into the earth physically. It is a portal that leads to a different dimension.

Much of the knowledge of the black skin people race on your earth is a lie and is hidden as well. Truth will be revealed in the next 2 generations to those who will remain here.

You are all children of the mother, but many of the tribes have been used by dark wizards, later in your timeline, as we have. So much pure magic knowledge has been given to the people on your land you call Africa, but it has been hidden, forgotten and distorted. Power has been taken systematically from the people of that land because they hold a high level of magic capacity and their numbers and size of their lands are larger than any other.

Much of your mythology holds truth, like dragons, middle earth, the library, dark magic, light magic, wizards and witches, priestesses, and evil kings. Worlds and dimensions different from yours and the travel between them, the knowledge of time and space, demons and temples, angels, and dark lords.

So much truth hidden and so much distorted.

There is a reason these stories keep being told always in many ways. Stories are the language spoken to us through the subconscious mind of the collective. A language that communicates with us, through us, through time and space, holding the truth that cannot be spoken directly.

The number 666
ONLY use it when your body is pure and you are using it in a sacred union, which we are aware is rare in your world. This is the only way to use it, after an initiation, in order to reverse its powers back into the light. If you use this number in any other way, it will damage your field. (We gave the same warning about the Merkabha. you MUST use it with the purest of vessel and intention).

You can read more about numbers, symbols and the sisters in: Symbols of Sex Magic.

DE-CODING STORIES

The story tells that 'king' Solomon built the temple. He didn't. He destroyed the original temple and took over the most sacred place on the continent of what your history books may call Atlantis, but truly was called Shahara. There is no need to confuse you with these details because we are simply trying to focus your attention on what truly matters. On de-coding the stories, the lies, into truth.

It is known in Jewish Talmud and midrash that Solomon used the king of demons - Ashmedai, to build his temple. He harnessed and used the most ancient demonic force to destroy our temple because no force was strong enough to do that. Of course, he also had to manipulate the hearts of the loving sisters.

Solomon captured Ashmedai with the power of the sisters. He couldn't have done so without their blood, magic, and sexual life force, which he took by force and pure malice and cruelty. The demons showed him he would need to use cruelty to extract this force from the sisters which hold the true power, since it is extracted from the womb itself, as well as other resources we will not share here because we do not wish to share the true secrets of this extreme baneful magic, knowing they will be used again in this way.

Ashmedai later tricked Solomon (as demons always do) and banished the protective layers he had placed around him and took away his powers. This took time, years in fact, but eventually Solomon had an army of men to protect him, though they were all killed, hurt, or manipulated by Ashmedai. The ridiculous sense of entitlement and the thought he was more powerful than the oldest demonic force brought his demise at the end.

Until today, Jewish people still call the name of this entity, and they think they call God. Endless times a day, they mention this word without knowing they keep feeding the same dark force Solomon conjured and with that, they keep feeding the world he brought once the temple fell.

This word is Ashem- but they say it as Hashem. Still, the sound is the same, and the seed of magic is as well. But they really refer to Ashmedai. Ironically, one with a pure vessel can speak any demon name and never be influenced, because despite reciting the codes (the name), the demon is on a completely different frequency and cannot reach the one calling its name.

The way that Solomon tried to save his name for generations to come, since he could see (through the magic of the temple and the sisters) many future timelines and he began the detailed work of organizing the exact timeline he wished to evoke. One of the things he made sure humans will remember as a fact (but is in fact a blunt lie) is that Lilith is the wife or counterpart of the demon 'king'- Ashmedai. To save his name, he made sure to taint the names of LILITH herself and the sisters, by distorting the nature, power, and divine gift of women and womanhood. You see. Demons will not remain alive forever, but the highest pure source LILITH was that Solomon attached to the demon's name, kept his memory alive. It is the power of pure feminine that gives life. That IS true power. His evil magic is still at work today, as we witness a society that keeps creating new ways to try to destroy, distort, and taint the feminine and LILITH within us all.

This will be in vain, though. The goddess can never be destroyed. LILITH can never truly be forgotten and the power and truth of the feminine, the womb and our sacred blood are inherited in our cells, in our cellular memory, no matter how many layers of muddy lies we have endured during all these generations. The mother herself is in all of us. We come from her source womb and we all shall return there. This is the magical gift that the temple is now restoring in our hearts and psych.

It will take a few generations for this truth to truly take hold in our world. This book is just a seed, but the mother is patient. The temple is eternal and no matter what, we all shall return home.

PART 4

GOLD

WE ARE GOLD

In the days of the temple, where some could in fact levitate above ground, the amount of pure gold was high in our DNA. I know this sounds fantastical, so I remind you to read this as a 'story' and let your all- knowing subconscious mind assimilate the truth into you.

We all have a small amount of gold in our bodies, because it is in our DNA, from our ancestors and it CANNOT be corrupted. No matter how much the dark forces have tried.

Nature still holds a high amount of pure gold within it. This is why it has been proven to heal faster and be healthier than humans, and why humans heal better in nature.

More gold = more oxygen, the ions from natural waters can help the absorption of gold into our cells. The problem is that our bodies are so toxic that they cannot absorb gold anymore. Very few can, especially those who eat small amounts of only raw, plant diet, but even they can only absorb a very small amount.

We have been forced to move away from nature. To live in an unnatural city environment which weakens the body, forcing us to de-volve into something that we cannot bounce back from.

The black sun cult, which with their distorted black magic, inverted and manipulated the power of gold and the sun in the mind of humans, has taken lots of the pure gold into vaults, but the gold is within us. A small amount still remains in our DNA. They cannot extract it no matter how much they try or manipulate it! They can only affect how it is absorbed in our bodies, and they in fact have done a fine job at it with synthetic foods, vaccines, as well as religion, and the media which constantly programs the psych of humanity.

We must follow the path of true initiation to unlock the keys of gold within us.

All life on earth has a partnership with mitochondria and it exists in every cell in our body. It powers the cells of the body. It is the light body of the cell that powers the cell. It has the highest concentration in the heart and in the 3rd eye part of the brain, which functions like a heart, and it has a type of heart cells within it. It is also abundant in the womb, especially after a woman has given birth, since the amount of information exchange with her baby is more massive than any scientific brain can prove. Another reason why the umbilical cord should never be cut. It still holds this information to the baby after birth, which is necessary for his life's journey.

Your family DNA is stored in the mitochondria.

It is a sort of blood code. Of cellular memory.

This is the connection to not only the core of who you are on all levels, but to source itself, which is also in all other life. You are literally connected to all life and source through your body as well as to all YOUR other lives and timelines.

PRIMA MATERIA- the prime material must be taken care of first. This is why initiation begins with preparing the vessel, the body, for higher levels of consciousness and information.

You cannot ascend without the physical body! The body itself has a technology which must be understood and respected, along with understanding the unseen realms and other dimensions we are in constant life with.

If your body is not ready, you will NOT receive the records, information, and light codes you are meant to.

It is that simple. You can end up at the gate of the temple and have no connection. You also risk connecting to other energies that are not high or wanted, which is what happens to most people which try to connect to spirit while their bodies are clogged and tainted with low frequencies.

This is what is happening daily, because most humans are in such a low frequency, especially when consuming animals and animal bi-products, alcohol, or ego driven drugs. Even people (and I see this all the time), that consume amazing plant medicine will have an illusionary encounter with what they think are high frequency entities or information and they are in fact opening portals they can't and don't know how to close. They invite energies into their realm that will remain there long after that experience. Energies that not only affect them, but the whole world. There are only a handful of true 'shamans' in the world today that will not allow any plant medicine before the body is fully cleansed and the people eat a plant-based diet. This is vital, and these are the only shamans you should trust.

Some people are so degenerate that not only they are not able to hold any higher frequency and information, but even if we fill their body with pure gold, it cannot hold it.

Science has confirmed (although it has merely scratched the surface) that particles of gold do similar things that the sun does, so imagine the explosions of sun energy that is in the human body when it breathes pure gold particles all day. This is what superhuman stories tell us about. We ARE the sun, but this power has been destroyed on this planet. All its natural power is taken from us and the earth.

The sun bonds us to the gold and the gold bonds us to the sun. This is a gift only gold offer. It is a super conducting prime earth material. Transmitting more energy and makes our body, senses, and consciousness (in past, present and future) more coherent. It is aligned on all levels and keeps us the same. It keeps shining into our body as well as emanating outwards.

Pure gold doesn't corrupt.

Gold has been manipulated to be used against us, like the knowledge of magic, our sexual powers, and the power of our voice (in spells and magic). Gold has been taken and depleted from us, its influence reduced while our mind manipulated and consciousness distorted, but we all have gold within us. No matter how low the amount is.

They were preparing the Prima Materia for invasions when they did that. Making the human body weaker and more susceptible to any changes.

One of the reasons the dark forces came here is to harvest the gold and, with the gold, the human soul and life force itself. For the life force is in the blood and the blood was in high levels of gold. Blood holds information and the gold in it and in the cells of our DNA, held the highest information in its purest form.

Imagine how powerful humans really are, that they had to strip us all from this power.

In the past, we had more gold particles in the atmosphere, in higher quantities. Gold was like a super conductor of energy. It was in the water, ecological system, all animals, and humans. There are some records of this in ancient Egyptian and other texts, most texts and records of this truth are kept by the church library. This is something no one knows about, until now.

When we had more nano particles of gold, we had more oxygen on this planet. The liquid gold in the water made the water to be of high healing and rejuvenation, cleansing abilities. Like the waters that surrounded the temple itself.

I wish to be clear that this gold is not what you refer to as ormos or nano-atomic gold. This gold is pure and powerful and is held mostly by the dark wizards on this planet, but it is also in our bodies in small amounts, which are enough for us to awaken and keep charged, if we keep our bodies in a pure state, as well as connect to the sun.

The state of the ecosystem now, within and without us humans, is far from being at its highest, best state. This affects not only our physical bodies, but energetic body, as well as level of consciousness, which affects the amount of information we can receive and grasp, the level of heart connection we can create with one another and other living beings, the ability to regenerate our cells, which of course include our brain cells, etc...

Gold is an element which is incorruptible, therefore, when we have high levels of it in our system, WE are as well-incorruptible.

This is why the hidden temples have high amounts of gold within their walls. This doesn't only keep them at the highest frequency but safe because as human frequency is lowered, they become less and less able to see and know about the temples, because they are not at the same level of frequency. This is why humans cannot find the real temples of ISIS & LILITH. They have been kept safe and hidden for fear of being found again by the modern dark wizards. Their protection is mainly important now at the time of the end of the cycle. The cycle began with the fall of our first temple.

Gold connects us to the tree of life. To the same dimension it exists in. Space that is often called Eden. A dimension closest in frequency and information to source. As close as can be yet still within the realm of manifested reality (This is how the sisters explain it).

This energy can give us access to our original template, blueprints, and light codes.

I want you to remember this- you have the same power and ability that Solomon had. The question is how will you use it? Although humans have lost the ability of levitation and other forms of direct magic due to the lowered frequency by baneful magic of your earth, you can still use your immense powers in new ways. You can use your voice. Your sex. Your mind!

You are each a microcosm of the cosmos itself. You each hold the codes and information of the cosmos itself. It is when you focus on your highest timeline and do not allow the constant distractions of fear into your body, when you can fully begin to shift and shift others with you eventually.

Be loving, gentle and kind to yourself. You are enough as you are now and always have been. You are a child of the divine mother.

MY JOURNEY

I wanted to share a bit of my own personal alchemical journey in hopes of offering you another layer of inspiration.

The sisters explain to me that gold is the sun. It is a 'gift' from the sun, given to this world, as well as many other worlds who have the same sun as we do. This is the reason why their world's destiny is intertwined with ours. Only a fracture of these worlds is known to our rulers (governments, elites, etc...) but they cannot be reached with our modern technology, as well as with our lower state of frequency. A handful of people managed to communicate with these worlds in other ways, such as evolved psychic gifts. The way I channel the sisters and communicate with the dimensions of the temple is a different story. I myself have not contacted those other worlds we share a sun with.

Gold is the 'lower sun'. As above - so below.

When we can hold more gold frequency (and sun frequencies) we can be more coherent, aligned, connected, and do our work better. We can connect to multiple dimensions, as I am connecting to the temple, this reality, and multiple timelines when I work in initiations or when I channel this information.

I had to (and still do) prepare and keep my vessel pure, as well as my heart (which is a constant work of the highest integrity) in connection to receiving and holding the golden frequency of sun, life, and love.

Gold alchemizes itself and offers us the gift to create alchemy within, as well as without.

When I initiate more women, when I help more women hold this frequency as well, together, as we are in the sun-bonds of our golden frequency connection, we become so much more powerful. We can feed each other, receive higher, stronger light codes, and change the energy field of all of us through our womb and Blood code activation.

Golden heart- field ceremony

Heart- field knowledge. This is what the temple offers.

Activation of the heart intelligence is vital, without it, any intelligence is empty. No matter how pure and clean the body is, if the heart is not activated, there can be no true communication with source, or with the temple within. There can be no sacred union.

Accessing the golden consciousness within us is a vital part of the entire initiation, which requires a lifetime of commitment.

Limitless sun energy is offered to us, but we do not know how to truly receive and activate it within our cells and hearts.

Sun- bond energy field with our heart space is always flowing to us but as our hearts are clogged, sick, hurt, disconnected, the golden information cannot be freely moving from sun to sun (this world and others who share the same sun) and from heart to heart (from each human to other living beings). We became truly disconnected.

Connecting our hearts with the sun and its golden promise will allow us to connect to each other and transmitting to each other as well.

Only when the body is not healthy and not able to absorb high frequencies of light you cannot bond and connect to this transmitting of energy from life. When we are at this level where we can absorb light frequency from all around us, this mineral that is also powering our mitochondria, powering our light body and that can have every sun-bond and frequency of light through us, constantly superconducting, never losing power or corrupting.

This is why the more I am able to connect to this energy, the less I can connect with people whom their body is not at their highest level. We literally 'don't speak the same language'. Our inner suns cannot bond anymore. For me, it may be more apparent than them if their body is at a lower frequency. They may think I'm a snob who doesn't want to be their friend anymore, but it is that our cells cannot bond anymore. Literally.

Protection also has a lot to do with activating the heart, so, with the magician's circle and an activated heart, you are fully protected. But this must be mastered. It involves all initiation, body cleansing- for it is your vehicle of light, where the heart is the center of life flow, and if it is not pure for light to flow through it, other lower energy will.

You are a portal.

You are a masterpiece.

You are powerful beyond logic.

You are pure alchemy, born from the womb of the mother, always loved, safe and protected, and to her womb- you shall return.

We Love You.

And so, as I, the last priestess of the original temple, am about to seal the pages of this portal, I remind you that although I was once the last, I am not merely the first. Join me sisters, on our journey back to love. To the mother, to each other, to ourselves. To the womb that calls us all back home.

A LOVING NOTE TO MEN

I do not wish for you to end this journey with the feeling or thought that the masculine is doomed. That the only path you are destined to take is that of Solomon. The masculine is not damned!

If I had believed that I would have no reason to do my work. I would have no reason to remain on this plane. I have seen the true beauty and power of men in their truth. Their divinity.

The original blueprint of the masculine frequency is of the divine masculine. It is sacred. You are sacred. You emerge from the womb, so how can you be anything less?

You have just been made to forget.

The divine image of the masculine which more and more women now hold in our hearts is of heart centered strength. Power that is more magnificent and able than any of a dark wizard. You see, wonderful brothers. Just as myself and many women remember who we truly are, so are many of you. you may have less ability to relish in the fantastical realms of your inner truth, you may not use your imagination as much as we are because being a masculine creature offers you a different gift or logic, mind and groundness use your grounded presence and connect to your heart. many of you will also hear the call of the temple to return to your original codes of sacredness. it will be a unique path for each of you, but as you surrender to the mother once more, even if you cannot rationalize these feelings or pull you experience, simply trust in your heart. the mother, as the feminine, cannot be explained. she is pure chaos of life and death and all that's in between. She is endless. How can you make infinity logic?

just like the symbol of the circle or the ouroboros, everything flows in its perfect dance of existence into a constant completion of another cycle, which will never end... we will emerge from the womb, and to there we shall return. We have no choice. We are all the mother.

I honor you brothers. The temple calls your heart to awaken once more from a dark spell into a song of your sisters. Those of us who walk the path of the temple, await you with open arms.

we know we are safe in your hearts, and you will forever, be safe in our wombs.

AS A SELF-PUBLISHED AUTHOR, YOUR REVIEW ON AMAZON WILL BE HIGHLY HELPFUL AND APPRICIATED. IF YOU ENJOYED THIS BOOK AND FEEL INSPIRED, PLEASE LEAVE YOUR THOUGHTS ON AMAZON (OR EMAIL THEM TO: MOTHERISRISING@GMAIL.COM)

WHAT ARE YOUR IMMIDIATE THOUGHTS, MEMORIES, FEELINGS, IDEAS THAT RISE AFTER READING THIS BOOK?

PERHAPS YOUR OWN STORY WISHES TO EMERGE FROM THE SHADOWS?

THE SEX MAGIC SCHOOL OF ISIS & LILITH

BOOKS

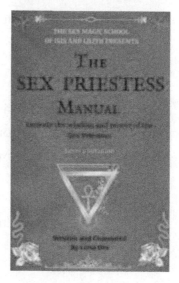

PROGRAMS

The Sex Priestess Initiation

The Goddess Return

The God-Man program

THE GODDESS
JOURNAL

A guided journal for the
awakening Goddess

By Luna Ora

CLASSES

Candle Sex Magic

Golden womb path for initiates

Creating Magical Children

And more to come…. With your support and Love I can do my work better in serving you, my brothers and sisters, and above all- in serving the divine MOTHER.

www.motherisrising.com

Made in the USA
Las Vegas, NV
13 September 2024

95221622R00075